Fly-Fishing for
TROPHY TROUT

JIM TEENY

BRENT CURTICE

Fly-Fishing for
TROPHY TROUT

BRENT CURTICE

Frank Amato
PORTLAND

JIM TEENY

"Give A Man A Fish and You Feed Him For A Day;
Teach Him How To Fish And Feed Him For A Lifetime."

Chinese Proverb

Published in 2003 by
Frank Amato Publications, Inc.
PO Box 82112 • Portland, Oregon 97282 • (503) 653-8108
Softbound ISBN: 1-57188-298-7 • Softbound UPC: 0-81127-00128-6

All photographs taken by Brent Curtice unless otherwise noted
Cover photo (left side): Jim Teeny
Cover photo (center and right side): Laddie Livingston
Illustrations: Bill Fenstermaker
Book Design: Tony Amato
Printed in Singapore

1 3 5 7 9 10 8 6 4 2

Contents

SECTION A. TROUT HABITAT 12

SECTION B. TROUT 22

SECTION C. FOOD SOURCES 34

SECTION D. EQUIPMENT 46

SECTION E. FISHING TECHNIQUES 60

SECTION F. SPECIAL SITUATIONS 68

Del Canty   Jim Teeny   Denny Rickards

Laddie Livingston   Bill Fenstermaker   John Welfelt   Dean Lampton

SPECIAL ACKNOWLEDGEMENTS

At this time, there are so many people that have helped me, I would like to thank each one, but the list would be endless. However, certain flyfishing masters, some of world renown, went beyond common courtesy to share their knowledge with me. They must be thanked.

Del Canty, a special friend. Del probably has more knowledge regarding fly-fishing, than any other person I've met. His stories and adventures always bring laughter and knowledge to those that listen. I thank him, for all the training and knowledge he's given me.

Jim Teeny, a great enthusiastic fisherman. Jim has more passion for fishing than anybody I've met. He's taught me more about the fine art of how finding and catching trout in a variety of places and conditions. He's truly a master fisherman. I thank him for sharing his knowledge with me.

Denny Rickards, a fisherman who truly perseveres. We've shared long days and late nights fishing for big trout. I am thankful for the fun we've had and the great times to come, I will cherish the memories. I am also thankful for his sharing of knowledge and expertise with me.

Laddie Livingston, my flyfishing partner. We've spent days of laughter in knee-deep snow and landing multiple trout with one net. He taught me how to think differently about situations. I am thankful for the memories made and the days to come.

Bill Fenstermaker, editor and illustrator. Bill is a superb fisherman. Bill is one of the finest artists in the country. I look forward to our future adventures. I am thankful for the knowledge he has shared with me.

My family, I am thankful for my wife and her compassion and understanding, allowing me to pursue in my passion of teaching fly-fishing. She's been a supporter, equipment hauler, promoter, counselor, editor, and friend. She's always there willing to listen to stories of how the big fish was caught. She truly is a special gift in my life.

My children, Chris and Amanda. I look forward to the adventures in the future we will share together as we bond as a family. It is their smiling faces that keep pushing me forward. I look forward to sharing many more family adventures together.

I would also like to think the following people for their expertise and memories: John Welfelt, Dean Lampton, John Duncan and John Parrott.

PREFACE

Sitting in Lyons Junior High School near Lyons, Colorado, where I grew up, I watched a fellow student tie a fly for a speech class presentation. The presentation was fascinating to me. I watched that student tie a fly, and I fell in love with fly-tying and fly-fishing.

As I developed my passion, I soon learned that the classroom became my home. "Teaching and fly-fishing go hand-in-hand." Patience is a prerequisite to succeed in either one. The ability and willingness to learn and never stop learning is the foundation that drives my passion.

I hold a master's degree in education from the University of Northern Colorado in Greeley, where I also earned a bachelor's degree in physical education and health. After excelling in teaching and coaching I began strive for more challenge as a principal of a high school. It is in the educational field that I unbridle my energy and capacity for achievement.

I've published articles in *American Fly Tyer* Magazine and *Patterns of the Masters*. I've been featured in flytying seminars all over the western states. I've taught flyfishing seminars and schools from Jackson, Wyoming to Telluride, Colorado. I also was featured in a video called "Three Days in the Gunnison Gorge," produced by Telluride Outside.

I began my teaching career and flyfishing guiding in Jackson, Wyoming. I guided there for six years. I spent one summer teaching a thirty-day flyfishing school to kids, based out of the Firehole Ranch on Hebgen Lake in Montana. I left Wyoming and Montana behind, and moved to Colorado, where I continued teaching and guiding flyfishing trips in the Gunnison Gorge for three years.

Today, I continue to guide on many rivers and private ranches and teach flytying and flyfishing schools throughout the summer.

The knowledge, challenge and patience of helping someone become better at all parts of flyfishing is an incredible and rewarding feeling. During the winter, I spend time teaching a flyfishing class for a local college. One of most rewarding opportunities is spending time working as a pro-staff member for Scott Fly Rod Company, Ross Reels and Jim Teeny Fly Line Company.

One of my earliest memories of fishing was catching a typical stocker rainbow as a five year old. I thought that trout was huge. Though many years later I've earned many world records in flyfishing for trout and have fished from Alaska to Mexico.

My true passion is inspiring children and adults to learn, whether that means learning to tie a caddisfly, how to dead drift a nymph, or how to solve problems. I've always been drawn to a career in education, because I love to teach. The school and the outdoors are my classroom. And that too, is why I have assumed leadership positions such as President of the Gunnison Gorge Anglers, the local Trout Unlimited chapter and helping with Huck Finn Days in Paonia, in which kids and parents are introduced to the world of fishing.

In today's world the availability of new materials for flytying and flyfishing equipment continues to improve year after year. The amount of information and equipment at our disposal is more sophisticated than any previous generation. The key tasks facing instructors today is exposing children and adults to new learning experiences that challenge and expand their minds.

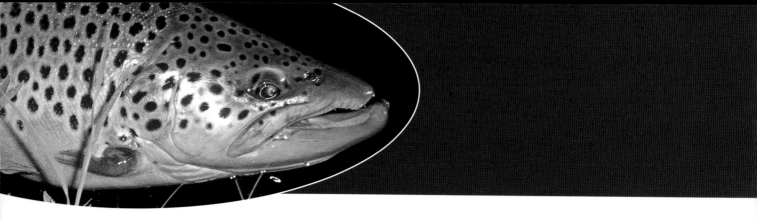

FOREWORD

Through my many years and travels in this flyfishing industry, I have been lucky enough to meet some truly quality people. Brent Curtice is certainly one of them. We met at a Denver sports show and I instantly knew that he was for real. People like Brent can only help when youíre trying to learn about the sport of fly-fishing. When we were talking he was so excited about fly-fishing, like a kid in a candy store.

That is the way it is when you love fly-fishing as much as Brent does. Our first trip together was in Colorado, at Dean Lampton's Bar ZX Ranch, for trophy-sized trout. Brent shared his knowledge of the many lakes we fished. To me this is a great quality that not many people possess.

He was excited for every fish we hooked and helped all of us in landing and carefully releasing the fish we caught. Since our first trip we have become very good friends. Brent is constantly giving of himself. His studies of fish and their habits, and how to successfully fish for them, are included in this book. If you are interested in expanding your knowledge of trout fishing, this is a ìmust readî. I have enjoyed reading his work and have picked up many new ideas that will help me on future trout outings. What is truly nice about Brent writing this fine book is his willingness to express and share his knowledge with others. You will be doing yourself a big favor when you sit down to read *Fly-Fishing for Trophy Trout*.

Good Fishing,
—Jim Teeny

INTRODUCTION

Why should I buy this book?

I am often asked, "How do I become a better flyfishing angler?" While it is a great help to talk to anglers, watch videos, read books and fishing magazines, there is no substitute for having a master instructor by your side.

My goal is to offer anglers a book to make their flyfishing experience a quality and memorable experience. Knowing that anglers want more than just a guided fishing trip, I have researched other books and resources on flyfishing to ensure that I am offering a quality book. No matter your age, race, or gender, this book will help you become a better flyfishing angler. I've taught kids programs, adult flyfishing classes, flyfishing schools, and continue to guide on a regular basis. I have a passion for teaching. I was a teacher and coach for thirteen years and now a practicing administrator in public schools. The understanding of knowledge and how to apply that knowledge is a powerful tool. That is one of the reasons why I've written this book. Even though there are many ways to learn different techniques in fly-fishing, before you can be comfortable with those techniques, the angler must have a basic foundation of knowledge about the sport.

This book covers a wide variety of topics which have been discussed in one or more of my classes and clinics. Obviously, very few books can capture all the information that anglers need. This book provides you the basic information on fly-fishing. Use the book as a tool, write in it, and take notes in it. As you go to classes or clinics, take notes in the book. As an angler you can go to any chapter to start reading. Use this book as a resource of knowledge. The more you read and reread the chapters, the more you will gain. The objectives of this book are to improve your knowledge of trout habitat, trout behavior, entomology, equipment, and many other factors that effect anglers. Fly-fishing can be very frustrating as you begin, don't be intimated or feel overwhelmed. Take your time and move at the pace that is comfortable to you. If you watch videos, attend clinics, or read magazines, hopefully this book can help you better understand the information.

There are several stages anglers go through as they begin fly-fishing. Each stage is critical to the angler's psychological development. Not all anglers will go through all stages or even in the same way. The following are often the most common.

The first stage is the "self centered". Anglers want to catch their limit every time and eat everything they catch. The angler is easily frustrated by not catching fish. Almost to the point that if they don't catch fish, they give up the sport. This is a critical point of development for anglers, because if they don't move through this, fishing will never be a relaxing sport. Anglers in this stage are susceptible to all types of gimmicks that can be bought, looking for the magical cure.

The second stage is the "Know it all." At this time anglers try to impress others with their flies, gimmicks, and knowledge. Anglers spend a large amount of money on equipment to impress other people. You will hear these anglers use big Latin words to describe aquatic insects. Usually the angler thinks they are the next best thing for fly-fishing. You can hear this person yell across the lake, to let everyone know they have a fish on. They practice catch-and-release techniques for the first time. Catching their limit is still a high priority. Frustration easily sets in. In this stage anglers have many reasons why they didn't catch fish. Anglers begin to join different clubs to gain recognition.

The final stage is called the "Essence of fly-fishing". In this stage, the angler understands the importance of the conservation of trout. These anglers are often more impressed by the experience than the catch. They often spend more time trying to catch quality-size trout rather than quantity. Large sums of money can be spent in travel to far-off destinations. And appreciation of fine equipment and hand-tied flies also develops. In this stage, the anglers spend more time helping others become more knowledgeable about their sport. Anglers spend more time cherishing their experience and the friendships they have acquired.

As you find yourself going through these stages don't forget the most important part, the fish. Without the fish, we have no sport. All decisions should be based on what is best for the fish.

I hope this book will help you as you locate new fishing areas, giving you the confidence to fish all types water, at any time of the year. If one person retains or gains information of fly-fishing by reading this book, then I have accomplished my job. The sport has been rewarding to me and I hope to spread that enthusiasm to others. I wish you great success and fun adventures. Don't forget to take your kids fly-fishing or teach someone else's child.

Section A
Trout Habitat

Chapter 1

Understanding Water

There is no better feeling than walking up to a pristine stretch of water. You can sense the excitement of trout rising to your fly. I remember many times, as I made the first cast, how excited I was fishing in crystal-clear water. The fly slowly drops in the water and I lose sight of the fly because of the reflection of the surrounding environment. It's an awesome excitement.

When people think of a trout stream or lake, most people think of a clear, unpolluted body of water with prolific aquatic insect life. When in fact there are very few rivers, lakes, or trout habitats where all these conditions exist. The quality and size of trout depend on these factors. In this section, I will discuss the factors critical to sustain quality trout.

Water Fertility

Water's fertility, or level of dissolved minerals, affects the production of plankton, which is the critical factor in the aquatic food chain. Fertility depends on the water source. Spring creeks, limestone streams, and underground springs are usually rich in calcium carbonate, an important nutrient. A body of water that has excellent water fertility usually has more aquatic vegetation and produces more insects and grows bigger trout.

Water Temperature

All bodies of water that support trout have one thing in common: cold water. The cold water can come from a variety of different sources: springs, glaciers, or seeps. Many streams fed by ordinary surface runoff become too warm for trout in the middle of the summer, except in areas where the temperature stays cool all year. Some trout can survive at surprisingly warm water temperatures. Browns and rainbows, for instance have been known to live in streams where water temperatures can rise up to eighty degrees.

The water's temperature depends on a high-quality water source, but other factors that attribute to that success are the shape, gradient of the channel, and the amount of shade provided by streamside vegetation.

A stream is broken down into three parts: headwaters, middle zone, and lower zone. The Headwaters usually have cold water, low flow, and a narrow streambed. This area serves as a spawning and rearing bed for trout. The middle zone has cool water and is the most productive part of the stream. It has the best aquatic insect life, and the highest population of trout. The lower zone has warm water, the current is slow, and has a silt or sandy bottom. The lower zone usually supports a few large trout.

Gradient

Besides affecting water temperature, the gradient of the stream or lake influences the currents, current speed, and what the bottom of the stream or lake is made of. The higher the gradient, the faster the current.

The most productive trout streams have a medium gradient, usually a gradual current with a gravel bottom, therefore providing a high insect life and good spawning areas. Some mountain streams which have an extremely fast current could have a gradient of 15 percent. Above 7 percent, the stream needs many obstacles and holding areas to support trout. If a stream has a .5 percent gradient, the water is likely to be too warm for trout.

Shade

Streams and lakes require shade to keep the water cool and protect trout from predators. A stream or lake that is over-shaded will create too much cool water, which produces poor aquatic vegetation. You can maximize the trout production by planting or removing trees to regulate the amount of shade.

Stream Channel

The configuration of a stream channel affects a stream's water temperature, current speed, and habitat. A narrow, deep channel generally is the best. In a wide, shallow channel, water is exposed to the air and sun, causing the water to increase in temperature. Streams that meander have more diverse habitat than streams with a straight channel. The best shape of stream is one with many riffles, runs, and pools.

Other Factors

Streams can support trout when the temperatures are cold and the flows are medium. Low flows present the biggest problem in late summer. Trout that survive warm water are under so much stress that they do not feed. Underground springs provide the most stability and ensure minimal flow.

Another factor is clear water. Clear water allows sunlight to penetrate and promote the growth of plants. Clear water also helps trout find food more easily.

The last factor is pH. In most streams, the pH level is of very little importance. Trout can tolerate a wide range of pH levels, and can live in waters with a pH as low as 4.5 and as high as 9.5. However, Low pH levels resulting from acidic conditions have wiped out trout populations.

Chapter 2

Types of Trout Streams

There are many different types of trout streams: freestone, limestone, spring creeks, and tailwaters.

Freestone Streams

Freestone streams are the most common type of stream. They have three different types of gradients: medium gradient, high gradient, and low gradient.

The high gradient is fed mainly by snowmelt and surface runoff. The current is fast, with long areas of pocket water. Because of the short food supply, trout usually don't grow very big.

Medium-gradient streams are the most common type. They have moderate currents, and numerous pools, riffles, and runs. The stream bed is mostly comprised of gravel, boulders, and some pocket water. The best medium-gradient streams have many springs and clean, rocky bottoms that can produce large trout.

Low-gradient streams wind through meadows, bogs, and alpine meadows. They have silt bottoms, undercut banks, and deadfalls for cover. These streams are fed by springs, swamps, or melt water.

Limestone Streams

Limestone streams have two types of gradients, low gradient and medium gradient. The low-gradient streams have spring water, gradual flow, and the streambed is composed

Freestone streams have rocky bottoms that create swift currents.

Wading across moss-covered rocks can be very tricky.

of silt, sand, or gravel. The depth is fairly even. They commonly have overhanging vegetation.

Medium-gradient streams have some spring flow, moderate to fast currents, and a riffle-run-pool configuration. They are mainly composed of gravel, and boulders, that usually contain high amounts of aquatic insects.

Spring Creeks

Spring creeks arise from ground water. They have slow currents and crystal clear water. The water is very rich with nutrients which allows for the growth of lush weeds and heavy insect populations. Spring creeks produce tremendous numbers of aquatic insects.

Tailwaters

Tailwater streams are fed by cold water from the depths of reservoirs or lakes. They often hold large numbers of trout, many of trophy-size quality. They have stable flows, that allow the development of vegetation and aquatic insects. If there are numerous water level changes due to water release, this can limit the insect and trout population.

Chapter 3

How Water Moves

The reason trout live in different places on a stream or in a lake is due to the mechanics of moving water. To understand this concept, you must understand basic stream or lake hydraulics.

Current Speed

Current speed varies within the stream. The bottom area has slow currents. The water surrounding the middle of the stream moves at a moderate rate. Water in the center area will move up to four times as fast, as the bottom area. The reason a trout lies on the bottom to feed is because friction with bottom materials slows the current as little as one-fourth the speed compared to the middle of the current. A fly drifts along the bank more slowly than fly line, because friction with the bank slows the current.

Eddies

Eddies form both an upstream and downstream holding area. These eddies can be formed from obstacles in the stream. Eddies also are formed from bends in the channel, or islands.

Eddies can provide cover, food and oxygen.

Trout feed frequently in moving water.

Drop Pools

Drop pools form at the base of (waterfalls). Pool depth can vary depending on the distance of the crest of the falls to the water level. A deep hole can be created by the (waterfalls) making a good feeding lie, especially for large trout.

Undercuts

Undercuts along the banks of a stream occur because the current flows to the outside of a bend in the channel, and the channel becomes swifter, eroding the stream bank. At the same time, the current on the opposite side of the bank slows down, forming a sand bar. In most cases, the outside bends and eddies below the sand bars and islands hold the most trout.

Chapter 4

Stream Anatomy

Understanding how moving water shapes the river channels and learning where trout hide, feed, and rest, are critical to success in fly-fishing. In productive trout streams, the current creates a riffle, run, and pool. This sequence repeats itself throughout the river channel.

Riffles

A riffle has the following characteristics: shallow water, fast current, choppy surface, and gravel or boulder bottom. This part is commonly known as the rapids in a river.

Runs

Runs are deeper, have moderate currents, the surface is not as choppy as riffles, and the bottom is made of gravel.

Runs are areas that are highly oxygenated and have an active insect population.

Pools

The pool is deep, slow moving, with a flat or calm surface, and a bottom made of silt, sand, and small gravel. The pool is an important feeding area for large trout.

Fast water in a riffle develops a deep channel, known as the run. The current digs the run deeper, and the velocity of the current slows down, forming the pool. As the water gets channeled into a smaller area, the flow becomes more constricted and the current speeds up forming another riffle-run-pool sequence.

Underwater view of a riffle-run-pool.

Streams provide classic riffles, runs and pools.

Trout feed in riffles during the day.

Chapter 5

Lake Anatomy

Reading a lake can be a difficult undertaking to the untrained fisherman. It's very important to determine the physical characteristics of the lake. Lakes, just like rivers, have currents, holding lies, feeding lies, and prime lies. The better you become in observing the essential dynamics of a lake, the better success you will have. The following are important elements that contribute to where trout can be found.

Inlets

Inlets will usually hold trout because the stream entering the lake provides cooler, well-oxygenated water and good insect activity. Trout will line up from the point where the current meets the lake until it disappears into the depths. This area is considered a good feeding lie.

Outlets

Outlets can be a very good area for feeding trout. The currents draw insects above and below the surface toward the outlet. These areas can be considered feeding lies and holding lies. Trout in outlets will be very wary and may not be approachable until dark.

Channels

Channels are difficult to find. Channels are a hidden secret to catching trout in lakes on a consistent basis. Natural lakes will usually have a channel winding through the lake. Reservoirs will usually have old channels existing throughout the lake. Look for the following indicators: dark-colored water, depressions, or submerged structures.

Shallows

Shallows are considered water to be ten feet or less. These are the most productive areas in the lake. Shallows contain weeds, mud, sand, rocks, aquatic vegetation, and different types of depressions. Trout are spooky and on guard as they feed and cruise through the shallows.

Shoals

Shoals are submerged islands. Shoals have access to deep water and are good feeding lies for trout. They attract many aquatic insects, including small trout, crawfish, and various types of baitfish.

Fishing different lake zones can provide excellent results.

Springs

Springs provide the very best fishing spots. The water seeping from the ground usually is a constant temperature and trout like to congregate in this area. Springs provide trout with much-needed oxygen throughout the winter months. Springs combined with weed beds provide trout with food, cover, shelter, and oxygen. Springs are good prime lies.

Weed Beds

Weed beds are either submerged or floating. The submerged weed beds provide the most productive fishing. Nearly all types of aquatic insects, foliage fish, scuds, crawdads, and others are attracted to submerged weed beds.

Foam Lines

Foam lines are formed by wind and water currents. Insects become easy prey while drifting in the foam. The wind blows the insects into the foam where they become trapped. Trout feed in and around the foam.

Cliffs

Cliffs provide constant shade and cover for trout. Cliffs can also become a trap for flying insects that are blown into the rocks and fall onto the water. Trout generally hold very close to the edge of the cliff.

Drop-offs

Drop-offs can be very productive during the day. Look for areas that are darker in color. Many trout lie just off in the darker color area.

Submerged weedbeds provide cover, food and shelter for trout.

Cutthroat trout frequent weedbeds in search of food.

Chapter 6

Drifts

There are many ways aquatic insects move in water. I have seen drifting insects of enormous numbers. This type of insect activity sounds the feeding bell. Trout feed passionately and recklessly to fill their bellies. The following are different types of drifts that occur in lakes and rivers.

Constant Drift

Constant drift is a continual flow of insects throughout the water in a 24-hour period. Even though the drift will be heavier during different times of the day, constant drift involves all aquatic insects. Constant drift can occur all day and night.

Terrestrial Drift

Terrestrial drift occurs mainly during the day. It is not uncommon to find insects floating on the surface during the day. A windy day can ensure a higher level of terrestrial drift.

Behavioral Drift

Behavioral drift occurs during the emergence of aquatic insects, known as a hatch, involving midges, mayflies, caddisflies, and stoneflies. When a hatch occurs, insects drift along with the current. The behavioral drift usually peaks just after dark and an hour before dawn. During these times, trout will gorge themselves on food.

A drifting mayfly emerging from its shuck.

Wind Drift

In a lake, wind drift occurs as the wind blows insects across the water or by moving the water currents on the surface. There are other types of drifts that can occur at the same time. Trout are very aware of water movement on the surface and the feed it will bring.

Wind drifts during the day can provide increased trout activity.

Chapter 7

Lake Zones

There are three life zones associated with lakes; plant, dark, and-open water zone. Each zone has different characteristics that aid trout. If you understand the different zones you can concentrate your efforts during different parts of the day.

The Plant Zone offers a variety of food and cover.

Plant Zone

The plant zone (littoral zone) is the major feeding zone for trout. The plant zone is the shallow area where plants, weed beds, submerged weed beds, and other good trout-habitat occurs. The plant zone is the area that is less than 30 feet deep.

Lake zones can change depending on the size of the lake.

Dark Zone

The dark zone (profundal zone) is deep, dark water, usually 30 feet deep and beyond. Very little light can penetrate this depth. Fishermen should spend very little time fishing this zone. Trout move very quickly through this zone or are found at deep levels.

Open-Water Zone

The open-water zone is considered to be the middle of the lake, which the sunlight penetrates. This zone is directly above the profundal zone. Once in a while trout will move into this zone to feed on insects. It can be a very opportunistic time to catch trout.

LADDIE LIVINGSTON

The author hooks a large trout in the plant zone.

Chapter 8

Wind Currents

Lakes are considered to be stillwaters. When the wind blows, it makes currents, this is called wind drift. These currents only exist as long as the wind blows. Wind drift can have an enormous effect on the feeding patterns of trout.

Fetch

The speed of the wind drift and the size of the waves that are formed are dependent upon the speed of the wind blowing across the lake. This is called the fetch.

Scum Lines

Wind drift does not move the entire surface of the lake. The water flows in a series of side-by-side spirals. This pattern is caused by the rotational effect of the earth. Scum lines are created by spirals. These are fantastic places for trout to feed. Many insects get trapped in the scum lines.

Thermal Stratification

Thermal stratification occurs in spring and fall. Lakes change according to temperature and oxygen. The greatest changes in temperature occur during thermal stratification.

In spring when the water slowly warms, the top layers of water reach the same temperature as the water at the bottom of the lake. At this time, the water has the same density from top to bottom, the spring winds begin to mix the lake's layers thoroughly, bringing the bottom nutrients to the surface. This is called thermal stratification. When the ice breaks in the spring, the water temperature is usu-ally around 32 degrees. The warmer water from the bottom will mix with the cooler water, creating the same temperature throughout the lake at about 39 to 40 degrees. This can occur up to 24 hours after the ice is gone. Thermal stratification depends on the wind and temperature of the lake. Trout can be as deep as 30 feet, or in the shallows picking up food.

In late autumn, thermal stratification occurs again. This time of year the warm waters from the summer high temperatures eventually reach the same temperatures as the cooler bottom water. At this time the food and oxygen is re-circulated throughout the lake preparing the trout for survival during the winter.

Longshore Currents

Wind tends to pile up water against the downwindside shore. The water then flows along the shore and back to the upwind side of the lake. These currents are known as longshore currents. The currents do not stop when the wind stops. Once the water is moving it has inertia, it keeps moving. Many trout feed in the longshore currents.

Surface Temperatures

When the wind is pushing warm surface water to the downwind side, cooler waters are then circulated to the upwind side. This creates a temperature change in the water at the upwind side. You can use your thermometer to measure the water temperature as it occurs.

Surface temperatures can change quickly with an approaching storm.

Section B
Trout

Chapter 9

Different Species

Trout are considered one of the most popular western game fish because of both their wariness and their fighting ability. Like all other fish, trout become conditioned to flee for cover to avoid predators. What makes trout and salmon different from other game fish is their preference for cold water. Most trout seek water temperatures between 50 and 65 degrees. They usually only live in streams, rivers, lakes, and ponds that are fed by springs or snow melt. Learning to find trout using a thermometer will ensure your success.

The different species of trout are: rainbow, brook, brown, golden and cutthroat. There are many hybrid species and rare endangered species, but for the most part I will talk about these basic five.

History of Trout

As we become better anglers, it's important to understand the history of trout. All trout are divided into two basic families, or genus'; salmonoids (*Salmo*), and char (*Salvelinus*).

Because trout are coldwater-adapted fish, they are thought to have evolved in the Arctic possibly 10 million years ago. The climate of that region resembled that of our temperature zone, much like today. A prehistoric trout (*Rhabdofario*) left its fossil remains in western North America. It's not known exactly when or from what ancestors trout evolved.

Some trout hatch in fresh water and then migrate to the ocean to spend their adult life before returning back to their place of birth to spawn. Sea-run rainbow trout (steelhead) commonly follow this sequence. Although all trout species can have the characteristics of both sexes; for example sea-run cutthroat, brown trout, arctic char, brook trout and others, it's an incredible journey for sea-run trout to return to their spawning grounds.

The two major trout families today are *Salmo* which consists of native cutthroat, rainbow, redband and golden trout, plus the Atlantic salmon and the non-native trout,

The author releases an eight-pound rainbow trout.

the German brown. All of these trout spawn in the spring except for the Atlantic salmon and German brown.

The second trout family is *Salvelinus* which consists of bull trout, arctic char, Dolly Varden, eastern brook trout and lake trout. All of these trout spawn in the fall and are native to North America.

The families *Salmo* and *Salvelinus* are divided into species and sub-species by the following characteristics: coloration, anatomical differences, and behavior. Even today some biologists disagree on differences of certain strains of trout.

Due to the introduction of non-native trout and the manipulation of trout populations by man, hatcheries, transportation, and the introduction of various species from one place to another has occurred in our streams, rivers, and lakes. It is almost impossible to fine a pure strain or species of trout. Many people had very little concern for the fishery and different strains of trout, the belief was a trout was a trout. In the past century there continues to be increasing concern for different strains of trout and their future. In many places, great effort is being made to educate, so as to reverse the cycle of a century ago. The reason for this higher focus of fishery management is purer strains adapt better to native environments and have a higher reproduction rate, creating healthier trout that better handle today's problems.

Unfortunately, water quality and the environment have changed dramatically in many areas. The constant problem of pollution, lack of spawning beds, and impoundment resulted in only certain trout species surviving these conditions.

The only non-native trout in North America is the German brown. Shipments of 80,000 fertile eggs were shipped to Cold Water Springs Hatchery on Long Island, New York in the winter of 1883. These fertile eggs came from Baron Friedrich von Behr. A year later another shipment came from a hatchery owned by Sir Ramsey Gibson Maitland in Lock Leven, Scotland. The Loch Leven strains were introduced into the waters of Yellowstone National Park and are still present today. The Loch Leven strain has the ability to adapt to different water conditions and has become such a fierce predator that it has replaced many other strains in that area. The brown trout will become one of the predominant strains of the future due to its ability to survive disease and predators.

One of the first recognized species of trout established on the Pacific slope was the Mexican golden trout. From that species evolved the redband and rainbow, which later replaced the Mexican golden trout except for in very few small high-mountain lakes and streams. The introduction of the cutthroat to the Pacific Northwest has altered our fishery over the past one thousand years. The cutthroat reached interior waters, that denied later species of trout, creating impassable barriers.

The char being adapted to coldwater conditions, evolving from the Arctic remains of the last ice age, continue to exist in waters further north than other species of trout. Other species of char such as lake trout, brook trout, and Dolly Varden, are also found in southern areas.

The eastern brook trout was the trout that dates back to the beginning of the continent. It wasn't until the late 1880s that other trout species started showing up. The eastern brook trout was the trout that was credited for our fishing heritage. Despite its name, it did appear as a native trout west of the Mississippi. When the last ice sheet receded, there was a direct correlation between a small band of brook trout in southeastern Minnesota and northwestern Iowa, and the waters of Lake Superior. Many sources believed that the Great Lakes brook trout population was derived from this connection.

In summary, golden trout, probably one of the first native species, remain only in high-mountain lakes and streams today. The redband and rainbow established strong populations across the West. The rainbow is generally considered the West Coast native and continues to be found across the country. Brook trout, a native to the cold waters up north and all the Char family, are considered a native of the northern and eastern regions of North America. The lake trout is found in deep, cold lakes while Arctic char and Dolly Varden are rarely found anywhere south of Canada.

Trout are an incredible fish. They prefer habitat that is wild, clean, and can sustain cold, running waters. Trout have the power to thrill, and can intimidate all types of anglers. The trout is our true barometer with which we measure our quality of existence. Their behavior, habits, beauty, strength, power, and capability to survive, make this prey a truly worthy opponent.

Anatomy

The parts of the trout are the body, head, gills, gill cover, pectoral fin, lateral line, pelvic fins, dorsal fin, anal fins, adipose fin and the caudal fin or tail. The following is a brief description of each species.

Rainbow Trout

Rainbow trout have rows of black spots on their tail, back, and sides. Rainbows have a pinkish horizontal band and pinkish gill plate, with some black spots.

Rainbow trout.

Brown trout.

Brook trout.

Brown Trout

Brown trout have a square tail. Their sides are light brown to yellow with black spots and usually some black, red, and orange spots. There can be a white or blue halo surrounding the spots.

Cutthroat Trout

Cutthroat trout have a reddish slash on their throat. There are different species of cutthroat trout, each with their own markings. Cutthroat trout tend to have green to very gold-colored sides. Yellowstone cutthroat have spots above and below the lateral line. Westslope cutthroats have spots concentrated toward the rear of the fish.

Brook Trout

Brook trout have a dark greenish to blackish background. The sides have light spots, with some red spots with blue halos. Their back has a dark, greenish, wormlike appearance. The fins have a predominant white marking, except for the dorsal and adipose fin.

Golden Trout

Golden trout have golden sides with a reddish horizontal band that runs the entire length. The tail has black spots. All the fins have markings.

International Game Fish World Records

Below are the All-Tackle World Records.

Brown Trout: 40 pounds, 4 ounces caught in the Little Red River, Arkansas, 1992.
Rainbow Trout: 42 pounds, 2 ounces caught in Bell Island, Alaska, 1970.
Cutthroat Trout: 41 pounds, caught in Pyramid Lake, Nevada, 1925.
Brook Trout: 14 pounds, 8 ounces caught on the Nipigon River, Ontario in 1916.
Golden Trout: 11 pounds caught in Cooks Lake, Wyoming in 1948.

Formulas

The following formulas are used to measure a trout's weight, length, and girth. These measurements can be used for taxidermy purposes or catch-and-release records.

Weight: Length X Girth squared ÷ 800 = Weight
Length: Weight X 800 ÷ Girth squared = Length
Girth: Weight X 800 ÷ Length = numbered squared

Wild Trout or Hatchery Trout?

Too many fishermen believe that hatchery trout fishing is not true trout fishing. I believe that most conservationist

Cutthroat trout.

Golden trout.

anglers realize that without hatchery-raised trout, we would not have as many fishing opportunities.

There are differences between wild trout and hatchery-reared trout. A 20-inch wild trout is literally one out of a thousand; it is genetically the best that nature can select. The other 999 have long since been killed by disease, drought, flood, and predators. It is rare for wild trout to become the size of hatchery trout.

Hatchery-raised trout have the following characteristics as compared to a wild trout: less colorful, easier to catch within a few days of stocking, don't fight as hard, and very expensive to stock the 8- to 10-inch trout. However, the main complaint is that when waters are stocked, the hatchery trout compete for the same food as the wild trout. When hatchery trout spawn with wild trout, their offspring are generally less suited for the waters they live in.

In our world today, the trout fisheries would not survive without a stocking program, due to disease and lack of purity in streams. Because of the pressure caused by fishermen on public waters, more people are raising trophy trout on private waters. This will be the future of trophy-trout fishing. People will pay large amounts of money to fish for world-class trout.

Whirling Disease

Whirling disease is a parasitic infection caused by a microscopic amoeba that produces a spore. The parasite may not directly kill trout, but trout heavily infested can become deformed and exhibit an erratic circling behavior.

Laddie Livingston wins the battle with a double-digit rainbow.

Whirling disease has a two-host parasite life cycle that involves trout and another host, usually a common bottom-dwelling tubifex worm. When a trout dies, large numbers of spores are released and then ingested by these worms. These spores can infect trout in two ways. The first is by attachment to the trout's body, the second is by trout ingestion of the worm, where the spore is released internally. These spores are very hardy; they resist freezing, drought, and can remain viable for decades.

Most native species have little or no natural resistance to these spores. Young fry are at greatest risk because the parasite attacks their soft cartilage, causing nerve damage, deformities, and death. Once a trout reaches three to four inches in length, the cartilage forms into bone and is no longer susceptible to the effects of the parasite. Whirling disease does not affect humans. People cannot contract the disease by eating or handling infected trout.

Whirling disease is considered to be the major factor in the decline of rainbow trout populations across the country. At least 20 states have whirling disease in their waters. Brown and brook trout are not as affected as rainbow and cutthroat trout.

As an angler, remember the following guidelines. Thoroughly wash off any mud from waders, boats, boots, and other fishing equipment that could hold the spores. Do not transport any fish from one body of water to another. Do not dispose of fish guts and other parts in the water.

The author releases a hard-to-catch splake.

Chapter 10

Feeding Habits

During their early years, trout feed on aquatic insects, earthworms, crustaceans, and some adult insects. As trout grow they feed more on minnows, insects, mice, and frogs. In most cases, trout eat the eggs and young of most species of fish, including their own. How fast a trout grows depends on the type of food it eats, and also the size and fertility of the water.

Generally, trout in high-mountain streams usually grow slower than trout in farmland country. Trout have a slower growth rate in small streams than those in good-sized rivers. The larger the body of water, the more an abundance of food and shelter are available for trout.

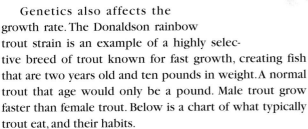

Genetics also affects the growth rate. The Donaldson rainbow trout strain is an example of a highly selective breed of trout known for fast growth, creating fish that are two years old and ten pounds in weight. A normal trout that age would only be a pound. Male trout grow faster than female trout. Below is a chart of what typically trout eat, and their habits.

Species	Common Foods
Rainbow Trout	Aquatic insects, vegetation, foliage fish, eggs, scuds, eggs, crawfish
Brown Trout	Foliage fish, crayfish, aquatic insects, terrestrials, eggs, scuds
Brook Trout	Aquatic insects, terrestrials, foliage fish
Cutthroat Trout	Aquatic insects, scuds, eggs, terrestrials,
Golden Trout	Aquatic insects, scuds, eggs, crustaceans

Spawning Behavior

The spawning habits of trout vary greatly among the different species. As a general rule, rainbow trout spawn in spring, brown trout spawn in late fall, brook trout spawn in early fall, cutthroat trout in spring, and golden trout spawn midsummer.

Before spawning, trout, especially males, undergo astounding anatomical changes. A male's jaw lengthens, with the lower jaw developing a large hook known as a kype. Their ugly appearance can intimidate predators and other males. Both sexes undergo extreme color changes. The color changes are different with different species of trout.

Trout prefer a clean gravel, silt, or sand bottom. The female digs a redd. She turns on her side and beats her tail against the bottom, moving the gravel. She tries to create a depression about as long as her body and half as deep. A female commonly digs several redds. She deposits eggs in each redd.

The dominant male will snap at other males to defend his territory.

During the spawning act the male and female lie side by side in the redd. They become rigid and arch their backs and their mouths open wide and then shake to release sperm and eggs. After spawning, the female covers the eggs with several inches of gravel. When the spawning ritual is over the pair of adults leave the redd.

Trout produce very large eggs but in low numbers. Trout eggs incubate for one to five months, depending on the species. A large trout (over ten pounds) only produces about 4000 eggs.

The eggs hatch in the gravel. After several weeks, the fry wiggle out of the gravel. After the fry absorb the yolk sac, they begin feeding on plankton. As the fry begin to grow, they develop dark marks along their sides. The fry are then called parr. All trout species lose their parr markings as they grow older, except for the golden trout. Predation is extreme during the trout's early life span. As a rule, less than one percent of fry reach the age of one. The chart below is a summary of spawning temperature and time of year when trout spawn.

Species	Spawning Temperature
Rainbow Trout	50-60 degrees/Spring
Brown Trout	45-50 degrees/Fall
Brook Trout	40-50 degrees/Fall
Cutthroat Trout	45-50 degrees/Spring
Golden Trout	45-50 degrees/Midsummer

Senses

Fly fishermen know that a sudden movement, a shadow, fly rod, or footsteps will send trout heading for cover. Trout depend mainly on vision to detect danger, but they also use other senses to detect trouble, such as: smell, sound, and taste.

Sight

Sight is the most common sense used by trout. Trout view the outside world very clear through a window. The window is a circular area on the surface, this window size depends on the depth of the trout. The best way to remember this is by the diameter. The diameter is more than twice as wide as the trout is deep. For example, a trout at a two-foot depth would have a window about four feet wide. The outside of the window is like a mirror to the trout, they can't see out. The light rays that enter a trout's window are bent, so the above-water field of vision is bent. Light rays near the edge of the window are bent and compressed; therefore objects at a low angle are highly distorted. If you stand upright and stay outside of the window of vision, the trout will see you. If you stay in a low position at the same distance, you will become distorted in the trout's vision.

Trout are also color selective. Trout see shades of color very well. When fishing with flies, try to match the fly with the closest shade of color that matches the natural. Trout have only fair night vision capabilities. At night it is best to fish with flies that have more movement and less color. A trout senses vibrations from the fly as it moves through the water.

What to remember when approaching trout:

1. Approach from behind and in the trout's blind spot.
2. Avoid wearing shiny clothing.
3. Keep a low profile.
4. Stalk fish during low-light hours.
6. Use smaller flies and lighter tippets on flat, clear water.

Understanding the way trout see can help you select flies and fish more effectively. A trout's eye is positioned

Sunrise or sunset can be a magical time for fishing.

to provide a large range of peripheral vision. Even though a trout has a large field of vision, there are several blind spots. According to recent studies, light is a major factor in fish behavior. When conditions become bright, the trout simply swims into deeper, darker water. As fish grow older their perception of brightness becomes more sensitive. Because of this sensitivity, bigger (older) trout prefer to lurk in dark areas and search for food in low-light conditions. As anglers, we often associate this characteristic with intelligence, when in actuality it is important for the survival of trout.

Smell

Trout have a very keen sense of smell. They use their sense of smell to determine food, detect predators, and locate spawning beds. Trout find trout eggs by the scent trail left. Bears and humans also give off a chemical that is detected by trout, L-serine. L-serine is given off by the human skin. Sometimes after you release a trout, the other trout will scatter because they smell the L-serine. I remember a time when the trout were feeding frantically, after I caught and released the first one, the rest just quit. They wouldn't even come around for a few minutes.

Sound

Experienced fly fishermen step very lightly when wading or walking along the banks. Trout detect vibration through their lateral line. The lateral line is a network of ultra-sensitive nerve endings along the side of their body. Sound travels through water as a compression wave, but since

Large trout can be fooled by an experienced angler.

A cutthroat trout caught in deep water at mid-day.

water is denser than air, these waves travel very fast and at great distances. Sound waves travel five times faster and five times farther through water. While playing a trout, the sound can cause other trout to investigate the vibrations.

Trout also hunt food by sound, because water is fluid and stiffer than air, sound travels through water as a rippling wave. Ripples die down quickly with longer distance. When fishing after dark, use flies that move in the water and create ripples.

Taste

Do trout taste their food? You bet! Trout don't taste their food like humans do, but they understand what their food should taste like.

There has always been debate regarding soft-body flies versus hard-body flies. Which is the best? There are flies on the market that are tied with hard materials, usually these flies look more realistic, but are less effective. I've found that materials that move, hold oxygen bubbles, and have other attributes that attract trout work better. Trout will take a nymph into its mouth then spit it out if it doesn't like the taste of it, or if the fly does not have some qualities of a natural. Always be careful of what is on your hands before you tie on your fly. Avoid any volatile chemicals like suntan lotion, oils, or any substance that can spread from your hands to the trout.

There are many ways we can control or even increase our odds of catching trout. Understanding trout and all their senses can only prepare the angler with better odds.

Chapter 11

Trout Behavior

The sound of a rising trout exploding for an insect is a thrilling experience. When trout are rising all around you, the frustration of not catching them can drive you to insanity.

When trout are feeding, you must learn to distinguish whether they are feeding on the surface, under the surface, or on the bottom. There are numerous types of riseforms both on the surface and under the surface. Trout act differently when feeding on the various stages of the insect's life cycle. If the hatch is a combination of insects, the ability to determine the riseform can improve your fishing success.

A helpful way to decipher the riseform is to notice if the trout leaves a bubble after the rise. A bubble means the trout is feeding on the surface. Take notes on the behavior of trout. If you cannot determine whether there is a bubble, use a small pair of binoculars. Once you have determined the riseform and made the appropriate selection of nymph, emerger, dun or spinner, you are ready for the next step, presentation of your fly to the trout.

When trout eat an insect off the surface of the water it's called a rise. By determining the type of rise, the angler can not only determine where trout are, but also what they are eating. When a trout rises for an insect, the trout then moves back to its holding lie, usually above or below the rise. Never cast a fly to the rise; cast at least two feet in front of it. The other information you can learn from the rise is what stage of the insect's life cycle the trout is

A big trout surface-feeds on an abundance of insects.

eating. This gives the angler a good strategy for which imitation to start with.

Trout that are feeding always face into the current. The trout drifts up to the surface of the water, examining the insect. When the trout eats the insect, they leave a noticeable ring in the water. Then the trout swims back to its feeding lie. There are several different types of rises, and I will explain each one briefly.

Sip Rise

The sip rise means the trout are feeding on the surface. The trout could be eating an emerger, dun, or spinner.

Head-and-Tail Rise

The head-and-tail rise usually means the trout are feeding on insects in the surface film. The trout will lead with their head and then roll, exposing the tail fin. The trout are usually feeding on emergers, nymphs, pupae, larvae, or terrestrials.

Splash Rise

The splash rise, where the trout completely comes out of the water, is caused by a trout chasing adult flies laying eggs or taking oxygen at the top of the water during a temperature change.

Tailing

Tailing is not a true rise because the trout is not feeding on the surface. When you see a trout's tail protruding above the water's surface, the trout is usually rooting for nymphs, larvae, and pupae on the bottom.

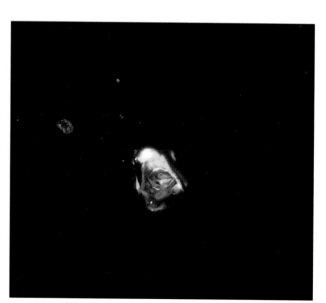

A trout opens its mouth to swallow a fly.

Chapter 12

Trout Lies

Trout live in different parts of a river or lake based on three needs: shelter, food, and protection. We call these places holding lies, feeding lies, and prime lies. Trout move throughout the day to different lies to satisfy their basic needs. Trout need shelter to rest. They cannot swim against a strong current all day, they would expend too much energy and die.

Trout live by a simple concept; the food they eat must provide more calories than the energy they expend to get it. Trout will fight strong currents and risk their protection to feed on large food items. Trout prefer places that have rough water, overhanging vegetation, or deep water so they can avoid being eaten by a predator.

Holding Lies

Trout find shelter from currents and protection from predators in holding lies. Holding lies can be found wherever the water is deeper than three or four feet and has some type of obstruction to break the current. Trout holding in these lies are very opportunistic, taking whatever food source is available. Common places are: deep holes that appear along banks, eddies below pools, and underwater springs.

Feeding Lies

A feeding lie offers a great source of food to trout. These areas contain plenty of drifting insects or bottom-dwelling forage fish. The depth is usually shallow, up to three feet deep. Trout will move into this area and feed, then move

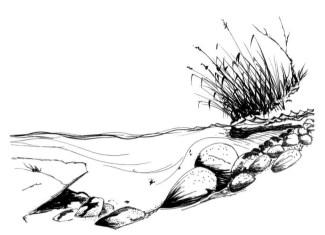

Trout will hold in overhanging vegetation.

back to a holding lie. Feeding lies also contain good oxygen content. Common places are: pocket waters, around boulders, current seams, weeds, overhanging grasses and trees, tails of pools, and riffles.

Prime Lies

Prime lies are the best lies for fulfilling all three of the trout's basic needs. Prime lies provide shelter, food, and protection. This is where larger trout will be found. Common places are undercut banks, pools, runs, and deep eddies formed by drop pools. The depth can be shallow or up to four or five feet deep.

Trout find shelter from predators under logs.

Trout hold in broken surface water while hunting for food.

Chapter 13

Feeding Periods

The more I concentrate on catching trout, the more I am convinced of how many different external factors play a large part of my success. Being cold-blooded creatures, trout are slow to react to and recover from changes to their environment, sometimes taking several days or weeks to adjust. The difference between feeding periods can be measured in minutes, hours, and days.

Weather and environmental factors will always be a large part of fishing, and the more we know about and understand them the more consistent we will be.

Water Temperature Swings

Trout and aquatic insects are affected by changes in the water temperature. Water temperatures are the key to trout behavior, and changes in those temperatures, no matter how small, are responsible for their level of activity.

Fishing success can be altered by as little as one or two degrees. The greater the change, the longer it takes for a trout to adjust. The impact of temperature change makes it difficult, if not impossible, to predict trout feeding and movement patterns.

During summer, for example, water temperatures reach their highest usually from 3:00 to 4:00 p.m. A lake or river's water temperature is greatly influenced by elevation, depth, feeder streams, creeks, springs, location, and the time of year.

Day or Night

Trout feed both day and night. Big trout prefer night feeding for several reasons: there is more protection in the dark,

An approaching storm can cause increased trout activity.

aquatic insects are generally more active at dark, and there are fewer flying predators at night. Due to the lack of predators, trout also have a tendency to cruise closer to the bank at night looking for food.

Trout will feed during the day due to the aquatic insect activity. Big trout are very wary during daytime. Trout move in and out of feeding lies so they are not detected by predators.

Thunderstorms

A heavy rainstorm associated with thunder and lightning can be an excellent fishing opportunity. The reason is it cools the water's surface and beats in oxygen. Another reason is the number of insects that are washed into the water. I've seen the water temperature change several degrees in a strong thunderstorm. After the thunderstorm passes, there can be a high level of feeding activity that occurs. Do not fish if lightning is present. See the section on lightning.

Barometric Pressure

Storm fronts bring falling of the barometric pressure. Trout become very sluggish, non-aggressive, have little interest in feeding, and will usually hide until it passes. Most of these periods occur when the barometric pressure reading is under 29.8. The lower the barometer falls, the bigger the impact on trout. Stormy periods don't necessarily mean the feeding will change, but low barometric pressure usually does. However, while the barometer is falling just before a summer thunderstorm, trout activity can approach very aggressive feeding levels. Once the barometer is above 30, the trout begin to feed normally again. Fishermen can use a barometer to predict the level of fish activity. The following is a good guideline to remember: below 29.8, very slow to nonexistent trout activity; 29.8 to 30.2, above average trout activity; above 30.2 average trout activity.

Full Moon/Solunar

Does the moon affect trout fishing? What is a major or minor feeding period? When is peak fishing time? Does information about the moon help? As a guide and flyfishing instructor, these are common questions asked by students and clients. Some of the biggest trout I've caught were caught with the aid of the moon. Full moons can have a negative impact on fishing. During the full moon phase, and for several days after the full moon, trout become very tough to catch. I have studied moon cycles and solunar charts for the past ten years and found that the least successful fishing periods are during a full moon and two days after the full moon. The best time to fish full-moon periods is at sunrise and sunset. There are many exceptions, but don't spend the only time you have to fish during the full moon. A lot of outdoor journals and pro anglers endorse the effectiveness of moon charts and solunar data. John Alden Knight acquired details of 200 record catches and found that 90% were made during the New Moon. I have found very little data that presents a strong argument in using moon charts or certain solunar times with trout fishing. I have discovered information about what has changed my way of thinking using the moon data for trout fishing.

After many years of collecting my own data on the moon's effect on trout fishing I have developed the following conclusions. The first conclusion is, the moon alone does not have a major impact on trout fishing. The moon orbits around the earth, completing a full cycle every 29.5 days. The moon reflects light from the sun and creates no light of its own, therefore undergoing a change in appearance as it completes the rotation. At the beginning of each lunar rotation the moon is in a different phase. The phases are named: new moon, first quarter, full moon, and last quarter. The rise/set of the moon can be complicated to predict. During each month there is one day near the last quarter without a moonrise and one day near the first quarter without a moonset. There are formulas to predict the times of the moonrise or moonset. The secret is was knowing when the moon rose and set. I have seen trout start to feed during the middle of a hot, bright sunny day with no hatch occurring. The feeding occurred during a sixty to ninety-minute period surrounding the moonrise or moonset.

The second conclusion I've found is that the phase of the moon is important. The biggest trout I've caught were caught during the new moon phase. I book most of my clients during the new moon phase. During the first quarter and last quarter of the moon, fishing is fair depending on other external variables. I will explain the other variables later. The full moon has the toughest fishing conditions. This is the time you need to combine the Moorish or moonset data to fishing at the appropriate times during the day. I've seen the full moon rise in the evening and as the shine of the moon hit the water, the trout quit feeding, I mean shut down. They didn't start feeding again until the moon was covered by clouds or began to set. I have recorded many large catches of trout during the full moon and new moon and continued for three to five days afterwards. So if the New Moon occurred on August 11, August 11 through August 16 has great potential for trophy trout. During the peaks of the full or new moon, the window of three to five days after are probably the only time that the largest trout are truly catchable. Fishing during the rise/set of the moon/sun, during these certain moon phases is crucial.

The third conclusion is there is always good trout fishing at sunrise and sunset. The temperature is usually changing and many different types of insects are starting to hatch. Combine sunrise and sunset with moonrise and moonset and you get a golden moment in fishing. When these four factors occur within an hour of each other, leave work immediately and go fish. If you combine moonrise, moonset, sunrise, sunset with the peak monthly period, big things will happen.

My fourth conclusion is weather-related. A change in

Fishing during the full moon can provide frustrating days.

weather can produce very good results. Every day I am fishing or guiding, I take sample barometer readings throughout the day and I've noticed a good a result as the barometer starts to move. If the weather is ugly with a falling barometer around sunset, big trout move. If the weather change coincides with the moonrise, moonset, sunrise, or sunset, and the change with the peak monthly moon, great things will happen. This is truly your best chance at a trophy fish. I have caught many big trout during a fall or spring snowstorm that combined those factors, it is phenomenal.

Wind

Wind can drive a fisherman to the brink of insanity. Wind dissipates heat and cold, distributes oxygen, moves water surface, provides cover for trout, and brings trout to feed. I have found that I catch fewer trout in a north wind than any other direction. North winds are usually associated with cold air; therefore no hatching of insects occurs. Most north winds put trout down and activity becomes very slow. The north wind can change directions after time, so don't lose hope. Bring a compass along to determine the direction of the wind. If the wind is out of the north, go to lunch.

Water Levels

Changes in the level of water have a very unpredictable influence on the feeding activity of trout. Most water level drops can raise the water temperature and steal the oxygen trout need. Dropping water levels force trout to find new feeding lies and holding lies. Trout look for places that continue to provide food, oxygen, and shelter. Rising water levels can change trout activity, usually they become more aggressive.

Section C
Food Sources

Chapter 14

Trout Foods

Trout eat many different types of aquatic insects. Common insects are terrestrials, earth worms, leeches, scuds, crayfish, and foliage fish. There have been many articles written about the feeding habits of trout, but most of the time trout feed randomly. Trout are opportunists, taking whatever foods are available.

Ideally it's best to match the size of your fly to the size of the natural in the water. Nearly all aquatic trout food blends in with the bottom. When trout are selectively feeding, you must try to match the hatch by imitating the natural with size, shape, and color. The way trout feed and the foods they prefer vary among the different species of trout.

Mayfly (Order *Ephemeroptera*)

JIM SCHOLLMEYER

Characteristics

The development of mayflies progresses from egg to nymph to dun and finally to the spinner stage. Because the pupal stage is lacking in the development, their life cycle is considered to be an incomplete metamorphosis. Mayfly nymphs are crawlers and swimmers. The adults lay about 6000 eggs. Mayfly nymphs have several different classifications: clingers, crawlers, swimmers, and burrowers. The nymphs live on the bottom of the stream. During the emergence, the nymph transforms into a dun. The dun sits on top of the water with its wings in an upright position. The duns mate and lay their eggs in the water and then die. As they lay with their wings outspread on the water, they are called spinners. There are hundreds of species of mayflies in the United States.
Life Cycle: Egg, Nymph/Emerger, Dun, Spinner.

Habitat

Mayfly nymphs inhabit lakes and rivers, their survival depends on the aquatic vegetation, temperature, oxygen, environment, and food sources. Mayfly nymphs live in unpolluted water drainages. Mayfly nymphs are the most fragile of the nymphs. They do not flourish where there is pollution and drought. Mayfly nymphs prefer rocky or gravel bottoms.

Favorite Patterns

Nymph patterns	Hare's Ears, Pheasant Tails, and Princes, in assorted colors, usually in sizes 8 to 20.
Emerger pattern	Soft Hackles, emergers patterns in assorted colors, in sizes 10 to 18.
Dun patterns	Blue Wing Olive, Pale Morning Dun, Callibaetis, Trico, Adams, Pink Lady, and should be tied in assorted colors, in sizes 10 to 20.

Presentation

• For the nymph, use a slow steady hand-twist retrieve.
• Fish emerger patterns with a drag-free float or just under the surface.
• Fish the dun and spinner with a drag-free float and long leader.
• Fishing methods: Brooks, Sawyer

Midges (Order *Diptera*)

JIM SCHOLLMEYER

Characteristics

The order *Diptera* consists of mosquitoes, house flies, black flies, craneflies, and hundreds of species of midges. Midges are known as Chironomids and can be the number one food source for trout in lakes.

Midge larvae are worm-like in shape and movement. Their colors are very diverse, ranging from black, white, red, amber, purple, olive, and brown. Midge larvae feed on vegetation, living animals, or non-living organic matter. Some species are known to be carnivorous.

The two factors which most likely determine the emergence are; temperature and length of the day. The life cycle consists of the egg, larva, pupa, and adult. After emergence occurs, oxygen becomes a critical factor. It's believed that oxygen gets trapped in the skin, helping split the pupal shuck, aiding in the emergence of the adult. Adult midges can be seen in swarms on top of the water after emergence.

Life Cycle: Egg/Larva, Pupa/Emerger, Adult.

Habitat

Midge larvae dwell in extremely diverse habitats. They are found in almost any type of water. There are more than 5000 species identified. Midges can be found in various depths, up to a hundred feet. Their favorite place is shallow to moderately deep water. Most midges can be found burrowed in algae, rocks, weeds, mud, and sand.

Favorite Patterns

Pupa: Mosquito Pupa, Chironomid Pupa, Disco Midge, Marabou Midge larva, and the Serendipity in a variety of colors, ranging in sizes 10 to 24.

Adult: Griffith's Gnat and Mosquito in a variety of colors, in sizes 12 to 28.

Presentation

• The Sawyer Method will best represent a free-swimming larva. Be certain to retrieve the fly very slowly.

• Use the Heave and Leave Method with a strike indicator and let the pupa or adult just drift in the water, oncentrate on the strike indicator.

• Using the Dead Drift technique on top of the water, in the current, is also very productive.

Caddisflies (Order *Trichoptera*)

JIM SCHOLLMEYER

Characteristics

Adult caddisfly hatches are very prolific. The caddisfly has two sets of wings that allow for its erratic flight. The wings fold back over and along the side of the body, and are shaped like a tent or V. Most caddisflies have two very long antennas. The size of the adult can range from very small up to two inches in length. There have been over 1,200 species identified. The adult skitters along the surface of the water. The female lays her eggs under water and then dies.

The life cycle is egg, larva, pupa, adult. The larva builds a case from debris found in the water. Cases can be built of sand, wood, and other debris. There is also a free-swimming larva that does not build a case a free-swimming larva seeks shelter in plants and algae. The larva has six legs they use to propel across the bottom.

Because of the widespread availability of caddisflies, they are a common food item of trout. The pupa or emerger stage is the most common stage taken by trout. The pupa will rise to the surface and shed its sheath to become an adult. The pupal imitation should closely resemble the actual insect in color size and movement. A lot of attention should be given to the fact that the pupal sheath contains an air bubble that can produce a gleam of light. Trout tend to key on patterns that have this characteristic gleam.

Life Cycle: Egg, Larva, Pupa, Adult.

Habitat

Caddisflies are found in freshwater environments. The larva does not like extreme depths of over ten feet. The different species range in size and color. The larva prefers to hide in aquatic vegetation that provides shelter and forage. The larva will attach its rigid case to rocks and vegetation. Due to its lack of mobility, the larva cannot survive where the water fluctuates.

Favorite Patterns

Larva: Peeking Caddis, Hare's Ear, LaFontaine's Caddis Larva, in assorted colors, ranging in sizes 8 to 20.

Pupa: Deep Sparkle Pupa, Soft Hackle, Emergent Sparkle Pupa in assorted colors, ranging in sizes 6 to 20.

Adult: Elk Hair Caddis, Bucktail Caddis, King's River Caddis, Goddard Caddis, Stimulator, and Dancing Caddis in assorted colors, ranging in sizes of 6 to 20.

Presentation

• The Leisenring lift: a weighted fly is allowed to sink to the bottom and is then retrieved slowly to the top of the water.

• Dead drift technique: let the fly reach the bottom and then bounce along the bottom.

• Greased leader technique: grease your leader with a fly floatant and cast an emerger or adult across the stream without weight, and then mend the line up stream.

• Cast the adult across the surface of the water and skitter the fly along the top.

Stonefly (Order *Plecoptera*)

Characteristics

There are approximately 1,500 species of stoneflies known worldwide. The stonefly passes through three stages in its life cycle. There is an egg, which hatches under water; the nymph, which lives under water on rocks, gravel, and vegetation; the adult which emerges from the nymphal shuck and then flies onto trees, grass, and boulders to dry off and mate. The stonefly's life cycle can last from one to three years. The nymph goes through 10 to 20 molts in the course of development. At this point, the nymph is whitish in color and is known as an instar. Some species grow to three inches in length, and all species spend most of their lives in oxygen-rich environments.

Life Cycle: Egg, Nymph, Adult.

Habitat

A water temperature of 77 degrees is the highest temperature a stonefly nymph can stand. Stoneflies live well in water that is cold, high in oxygen, and with very little pollution. Stoneflies like to feed on moss, animal pieces, chironomid larvae and mayfly nymphs. Most stoneflies feed twice a day when the temperature is between 52 to 62 degrees, depending on the season. The roaming abilities of this species make it an opportunistic food item for trout.

Favorite Patterns

Nymph: Bitch Creek Nymph, Girdle Bug, Brook's Stone, Kaufmann's Stone, Halfback, Woolly Bugger, and Montana Stone usually in sizes 4 to 10.

Adult: Fluttering Stone, Sofa Pillow, Stimulator, and McSalmon Fly in sizes 4 to 12.

Presentation

• The nymph should be fished dead drift along the bottom of the river.
• The strip tease method can be very deadly.
• The adult should be fished dead drift on the top of the water with short, skittering movements.

Terrestrials

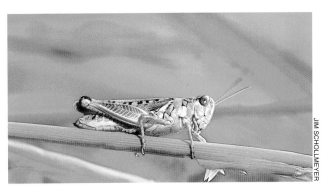

Characteristics

Terrestrial insects include grasshoppers, beetles, and ants. Most of these insects are blown into the water, or are washed into lakes and rivers by rain or runoff. Terrestrial insects have a life cycle outside of the water. Some insects can stay afloat for extended periods. Mid-summer through fall, you will find terrestrial fishing very effective.

Habitat

All terrestrials crawl on bushes, grasses, trees, and other obstacles on the water's edge. When there is even a slight wind blowing, many terrestrials are swept into the water. While considered little food for trout, under certain conditions you may encounter trout gorging themselves on terrestrials.

Favorite Patterns

Joe's Hopper, Dave's Hopper, Foam Beetle, Foam Ant, and Flying Ant in assorted sizes 12-20.

Presentation

• All terrestrials can be fished with a twitching action, strip tease method on the surface, or with a dead-drift technique. It's best to fish them in a feeding line, current seam, or next to overhanging vegetation, trees, or grassy banks.

Forage Fish

Characteristics

As trout continue to grow, small forage fish become a very significant part of their diet. Trout are natural predators.

Trout do not always attack small fish out of hunger. Sometimes they attack out of anger or curiosity.

There are two types of forage fish: bottom dwellers have wide bellies and live near the bottom. Some examples are: sculpin, darters, shiners, and suckers. The second type is: free swimmers, which are slender with oval bodies and live in groups or by themselves. Examples are chubs, whitefish, carp, and trout.

Habitat

Most forage fish live near the bottom of streams or along the shores of lakes. They find protection in large numbers, rocks, and vegetation. Forage fish are very erratic in their movement. They dart from rock to rock, or swim in schools. Trout will chase minnows to extreme distances to catch them.

Favorite Patterns

Muddler Minnow, Woolly Bugger, Matuka Sculpin, Platte River Special, Mickey Finn, Zonker, and Hornberg in sizes 10 to 4.

Presentation

- Cast weighted streamers up and across the stream, making short strips in the line.
- Skipping the streamer across the surface of the water.
- Fishing the streamer dead drift can also produce results.

Dragonflies and Damselflies
(Order *Odonata*)

JIM SCHOLLMEYER

Characteristics

These aquatic insects are two of the most common groups found in lakes, ponds, and some streams. They are very quick, with erratic movements as they dart in search of food. They have two sets of wings, operating independently of each other, allowing them the ability to move in reverse. Their body colors are a brilliant blue, green, and even brown.

Dragonflies emerge from the nymph to the adult. The nymphs are well armored with wide abdomens. They range in size, up to two inches in length. Water is taken through the anus for breathing, and when necessary, is ejected forcefully as a means of propelling the nymph. The

nymph has a nine- to eighteen-month life span. They eat any live insects or foliage fish.

Damselflies emerge from the nymph stage to the adult just like the dragonfly. Their life span is from three to five months. The damselfly is much smaller and varies in size from one-half inch to one inch in length, with a very thin, streamlined body. All damselfly nymphs have three distinct tails. When swimming, the nymphs have a rhythmic wiggle from side to side. The damselfly is also a predator, eating many aquatic insects.

Habitat

Both damselflies and dragonflies like shallow, spring-fed lakes with good aquatic vegetation. Both require pollution-free water and an abundance of oxygen. Dragonflies and damselflies seek out river inlets, drop-offs, and shallow areas where they can be found among exposed vegetation. They may even stalk their prey, instead of waiting for the prey to come to them.

Favorite Patterns

Damselfly Adults:	Adult Damsel patterns tied in blue, green and brown, ranging in sizes from 8 to 12.
Damselfly Nymphs:	Marabou Damsel and Beadhead Marabou Damsel tied in olives, browns, tan, and various combinations ranging in sizes from 8 to 12.
Dragonfly Patterns:	Lake Dragonfly, Assam Dragon, and Randall's Dragon in assorted colors, ranging in sizes 4 to 10.

Fishing Strategies

- Cast the dragonfly nymph and let it sink, strip line four to six inches at a time, then pause.
- Fishing damselfly nymphs is simply short one-inch pulls of the fly line with regular pauses. Try to imitate the wiggle of the body.
- Fish the adult pattern dead drift on top of the water with slight movement.

Leeches (Order *Hirudinea*)

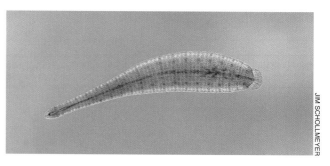

JIM SCHOLLMEYER

Characteristics

Leeches are worms recognizable by their flattened, elastic-like bodies and disc-shaped mouths. Leeches can grow up to six inches in length. Their colors range from cream, black, brown, and olive. They can have a lateral stripe, spots, or mottled markings. Many species are carnivorous, feeding on aquatic insects, earthworms, snails, and other creatures. Few species actually seek blood as their primary food. When swimming, they move like a flag in the wind and hang in a vertical position under the surface or crawl along the bottom.

Habitat

Leeches live in virtually all types of fresh water. They prefer shallow lakes and ponds that contain an abundance of bottom debris. They are nocturnal creatures that move through the water in the dark. They are available all months of the year.

Favorite Patterns

Woolly Bugger, Marabou Leech, Rabbit Leech, and Zonker in assorted colors, ranging in sizes from 4 to 12.

Presentation

- The best method is the hand-twist retrieve creating a long smooth motion.
- Another technique is to let the leech lie on the bottom for a second and then give it a short, sharp jerk, then repeat this motion.

Scuds (Order *Amphipoda*)

JIM SCHOLLMEYER

Characteristics

Scuds belong to the order of Amphipoda and the class crustacea. There are two types, *Gammarus* and *Hayalella*, which resemble each other very closely. Because of their great numbers and high caloric value, trout gorge on them. Many anglers refer to them as shrimp, but I refer to them as scuds. They range in size from one-third to one-inch in length. Scuds are found in many colors, including gray, olive, brown, cream, orange, red, and various combinations thereof.

Habitat

Scuds are found in small lakes, ponds, seeps, springs, and many rivers, especially (tailwater) rivers. Scuds cannot tolerate polluted waters. Scuds also live in high-mountain lakes and ponds. Waters that contain scuds produce fast-growing trout. Scuds seek out gravel, dead leaves, debris, and moss for cover and food. They can also survive in extreme temperature of cold to unusually warm water.

Favorite Patterns

Scud, Trueblood Otter ranging in colors of olive, brown, tan, or rose, sizes 10-18.

Presentation

- The best method is the hand-twist retrieve creating a short jerky motion.
- Scuds can be fished with a variety of techniques. Retrieve slowly and be patient.

Crayfish (Order *Crustacean*)

Characteristics

Crayfish are a freshwater delight. They are scavengers and will attempt to consume anything on the bottom of a lake. They may reach up to five inches in length. Crayfish only live one to two years. They are rusty brown and orange in color.

Habitat

Crayfish prefer shoreline areas, weed beds, bottom debris, roots, and snags. Crayfish are nocturnal; dawn and dusk are when they are most vulnerable. They also live in many lakes and ponds. Waters that contain crayfish produce big trout. They seek out gravel, dead leaves, debris, and moss for cover and food. They can also survive in extreme temperature of cold to unusually warm water.

Favorite Patterns

Crawfish patterns in colors of olives and browns, in sizes 4-10.

Presentation

- The best method is a hand-twist retrieve creating a short motion every 20 seconds.
- The retrieve should be very slow almost no movement.
- The best fishing technique is to allow your imitation to settle on the bottom, strip in bursts, making three to four strips, and then allow the fly to sink.

Chapter 15

Insect Collection

Many aquatic insects, whether they are nymphs, larvae, or crustaceans live in different types of water. The type of bottom and water speed is important in determining the type of aquatic insects you find. In fly-fishing there is usually a fascination with understanding the aquatic insects and their hatches. Collect insects to determine the size, shape, and color, so you can tie a close representation of the natural. You also need to know the habits of the insect and how to fish it in a natural manner.

Record Keeping

In order to gather nymphs, you need to know where each one was collected and keep some form of record. If you rely on memory, you will find yourself hopelessly lost. I emphasized record keeping at the start because I have found that unless your records are easy to use, you don't spend the energy to collect insects. The information you need is includes, stream/river, water type, water speed, bottom type, weed type, location, depth, insect name, and date.

Solution

A temporary solution for preserving insects is 80 percent rubbing alcohol and 20 percent water. Placing the insect in a jar of this solution will preserve it (Over time the insect will lose its color in this solution). Seal your jar tightly or the solution will slowly evaporate. After securing the insect in the jar, keep a record od its details.

Seining

You can acquire insects by seining from silt, sand, gravel, and rock bottoms. Push your seine into the bottom of the river bed, holding the seine as tight as possible. Then with your hands, shovel, stick, or feet, turn over the bottom material two to three feet upstream. When you feel you have collected enough material, raise your seine up and carry the seine to the river bank.

Collecting aquatic insects requires minimal tools.

Insect Collection Chart

Card Number_____ Name of Insect_____

Day_____ Date_____ Time_____

Specific Location:_____
_____

❑ River   ❑ Stream   ❑ Reservoir   ❑ Lake ❑ Pond

Temperature:

Air:_____   Time:_____   ❑ a.m. ❑ p.m.

Water:_____   Time:_____   ❑ a.m. ❑ p.m.

Water Conditions:

Level:	❑ Low	❑ Medium	❑ High	
Clarity:	❑ Dirty	❑ Cloudy	❑ Clear	
Speed:	❑ Slow	❑ Medium	❑ Fast	
Depth:	❑ 1-3 ft	❑ 3-5 ft	❑ 5-7 ft	❑ 7+ft

Location:

River:	❑ Riffle	❑ Run	❑ Pool	❑ Tail	❑ Other		
Lake:	❑ Inlet	❑ Outlet	❑ Channels	❑ Shallows	❑ Weed Beds	❑ Cliffs	❑ Drop-offs

Other_____

Bottom Type:

River:	❑ Silt	❑ Gravel	❑ Weeds	❑ Boulders	❑ Other_____
Lake:	❑ Weed Beds	❑ Shoals	❑ Gravel	❑ Boulders	❑ Other_____

Insect Activity:

❑ Mayfly	❑ Caddis	❑ Midge	❑ Stonefly	❑ Streamer	❑ Terrestrial	❑ Other_____
❑ Larva	❑ Nymph	❑ Emerger	❑ Adult	❑ Spinner		❑ Other_____

Observations:

_____
_____
_____
_____
_____
_____

Drawings, Sketches:

Chapter 16

Match the Hatch

A hatch occurs when a group of insects transform from the larval stage into an adult. A hatch can be very prolific, with hundreds to thousands of insects on the water. Obtain a specimen, then look in your fly box and try to match the size, shape, and color. This is called matching the hatch.

Selectivity is the ability to discriminate between different insects. Trout are very selective when eating, or are they? Trout will use as little energy as possible to acquire food. Contrary to what you read about trout, they prefer to eat the most abundant or recognizable food source. Trout make mistakes in feeding, because the only way they can switch from one food to another is through experimenting. Trout will select a variety of foods to maximize the number of calories they intake. The ability of a trout to inspect a pebble or twig and reject it as food, is the process of selectivity. The same idea occurs when a trout ignores your fly, if the trout does not recognize it as a natural insect, it will snub your fly.

There are days when trout will not come to your flies no matter what the pattern or your technique. But most of the time, when the trout seem inactive it's because they have been spooked or are feeding at a deeper depth.

First rule, always check the water temperature. If the water temperature is below 50 degrees, or over 70 degrees, trout will seek hiding lies, and may not be visible. If the water is at a normal level, and the water temperature is between 50 and 70 degrees, you have a choice of nearly any fly.

Second rule, if the water is high, cold, or very dirty, start with a streamer. The advantage of a streamer is that you can entice trout to the fly. It also gives you an idea of where trout might be holding. Be careful to present the streamer without spooking other trout.

Third rule, the more prolific the insects, the greater the chance a nymph will be your next-best choice. On a river, a nymph is a wise second choice. The nymph can represent many different types of aquatic insects. Over 90 percent of what trout eat lives under the surface. Start with a small size, 14-18 is generally a good decision. Your first cast needs to be your best, because more than likely you haven't spooked any trout.

Fourth rule, whether you are fishing with streamers or nymphs, start shallow and work down. Keep adding weight to your leader to get your fly deeper.

How long do you go before changing flies? I start first by changing the depth at which I retrieve the fly. Then try different lines and different retrieves before I change the fly. Your fly pattern must mimic natural movement so incorporate motion, like a breathing insect. Trout will focus on the size, shape, color, and motion of the fly. It's usually the presentation, not the fly, that attracts the trout.

The feeding habits of trout are determined by the number of calories eaten and the number of calories expended. During a hatch, there is a great abundance of food available, but hatches only last a few hours. Once the hatching insect becomes the food item, trout will usually ignore all other types of food. To take advantage of this feeding period, use the following process:

Determine what type of insect trout are feeding on (mayflies, caddisflies, midges, stoneflies, etc.). Then identify the riseform. Next, determine the size, shape, color, and movement of the insect. Finally, select the appropriate fly pattern.

If a multiple hatch occurs where two or more insects are hatching, even a veteran angler will have difficulty selecting the right fly. Remember the following guidelines: Trout usually feed on the insect present in the greatest numbers, and they choose the smallest insects that are available.

Multiple hatches can be frustrating and confusing, so don't be discouraged if your first attempts don't work. One of the most challenging aspects of fly-fishing is its complexity. To be successful during a hatch, remain calm and remember the process of selection.

Chapter 17

Flies

Most fly patterns are developed to imitate natural insects that are eaten by trout. All trout rely on aquatic insects at some point in their life. Some flies are tied very realistically, with markings, antennas, jointed legs, eyes, and other body markings. To catch trout, realistically-tied flies are not needed. There are five critical components that should be considered when selecting flies or tying flies to match the natural: size, color, shape, action, and materials.

Your fly should closely match the size of the natural or be a little smaller. The closer the color of the fly is to the natural, the better. Try to select a color as close as possible. A general shape or structure of the natural is all that is needed. I believe that action is one of the most important criteria. The better the fly moves in the water, the more the fly will entice trout to strike. Many times, materials are the final piece that triggers the trout to bite. Materials used to create the fly should have one of the following characteristics: movement, reflective capabilities, light gathering, or the ability to collect oxygen bubbles.

Dry Flies

When you see insects drifting on the water or flying around on the surface of the water, we call these adult flies or dry flies. Dry flies have distinct body parts, hackle, wings, tail, and a tapered body. Suggested patterns are: Adams, Royal Wulff, Royal Coachman, Royal Humpy, Humpy, and the list goes on.

Nymphs

Nymphs are flies that represent the larval, pupal, or nymphal stages of aquatic insects. Some nymphs also represent other aquatic insects such as, scuds, damsels, and dragonflies. Nymphs make up over 80 percent of the trout's diet and are available year round to the trout.

Suggested patterns are: Prince Nymph, Hare's Ear, Pheasant Tail, Montana Stone, and Bitch Creek. There are hundreds of different types of nymphs.

Wet Flies

Wet flies represent dead insects or emergers. Wet flies are designed to closely resemble adult flies that haven't completed the final stage of their life cycle. Wet flies have distinct body parts such as head, down wing, tapered body, and throat. Wet flies usually have the following characteristics; soft hackles, wool, chenille, reflective or absorbent materials. Suggested patterns are: Woolly Worm, Blue Dun, and a variety of soft-hackle patterns.

Streamers

Streamers represent baitfish, forage fish, and other larger moving insects. Most streamers are tied with the following characteristics: reflective materials, weight, absorbent materials, soft hackles, wool bodies, and extra-long hooks. Streamers have some common parts; body, head, wing, and throat. Suggested patterns are: Woolly Bugger, Beadhead Bugger, Crystal Bugger, Muddler Minnow, Matukas, and Zonkers.

Terrestrials

Some of the most popular summer flies are terrestrials. Terrestrials represent land insects such as ants, grasshoppers, crickets, and beetles, or any insect that may fall into the water. They are especially good during the summer months. Terrestrials are fished on the surface in a slow or moderate current and close to the banks of a river or lake. Most terrestrial patterns have some reflective materials tied in the pattern. Suggested patterns are: Dave's Hopper, Joe's Hopper, Whitlock Hopper, Foam Beetle, ant patterns, Dave's Cricket, Jassid, and beetle patterns.

Chapter 18

Buying and Selecting Flies

It's important for every fly fisherman to become knowledgeable about buying flies. You can spend a fortune and never get the flies you need. Remember these two important points: Not every species of aquatic insect comes off every stream. Second, it doesn't take millions of flies, or dollars, to do it right. There are a handful of different flies that will work almost everywhere you go fishing. The following are some guidelines you can use when buying or choosing flies.

Selection of Flies

The following are questions you should ask yourself before you leave on a fishing trip. Determine what type of fishing you are going to do. Make sure you know whether you are fishing rivers, lakes, or spring creeks, and then purchase your flies accordingly.

Find out the major hatches on the water you are going to fish. Knowing this information can save you a lot of time and money. Look for the local sporting goods shops or specialty fly shops in that area.

Carry flies you will need for the trip. The best resources are local sporting goods stores and specialty fly shops in the area. Also check out web sites that can give you information.

The following are standard flies that can help any angler, wherever you go.

Dry Flies:	Adams, Royal Humpy, Royal Wulff, sizes 12-20.
Caddis Flies:	Elk Hair, King River Caddis, sizes 12-16.
Nymphs:	Hare's Ear, Prince Nymph, Pheasant Tail, Girdle Bug, sizes 12-16.
Terrestrials:	Hoppers, size 8-14; Ants, size 14-18; Beetles, size 16-20.
Streamers:	Woolly Buggers, Zonkers, Muddler Minnows, sizes 6-10.

Buying Flies

Does quality make a difference? You bet! It's expensive to purchase flies, that's why you should get your money's worth. Too many times, people buy cheap flies and they fall apart before they go fishing, or after catching just one trout. When you purchase flies from a store remember these guidelines:

Uniformity

• Do all the flies in the bin look alike?
• Are tails and wings same length as the body?
• Hackle should be the length of the wings.
• Dry-fly hackle should be stiff. Try the bounce technique, drop the dry fly onto a table and see if it lands in the correct position.

Dressing

Look at how the fly is dressed?
• Head
• Too much on top (ex. hoppers), does the fly land on the correct side, when dropped.

Plucking/Pulling:

• Don't be afraid to pluck and pull the hackle, tail, and wings.

Color:

• Are all the flies in the bin the same color?
• Are bodies, wings, and tails the same?

Hooks:

• Ask an employee if the hooks are chemically sharpened. All good brands in today's market are chemically sharpened. A sharp hook can make a difference.

Imported or Domestic

Ask if the flies are hand tied or machined tied. Usually you get a better quality fly if it's hand tied by a professional tier. There are a lot of people who call themselves professionals that do poor work. Remember to use the steps above to determine the quality of flies.

Buying From a Catalog

If you purchase flies from a catalog, always buy more than one of the same kind. There can be differences in flies. It's risky to buy from a catalog, try to talk to someone in the store about the flies before you buy them.

Fly Mortality

One of the worst things a fly fisherman can do is not take care of their flies. Getting a fly out of a trout's mouth does more damage than a day of casting. Using forceps to pry a fly out of a trout's mouth can cause damage to the fly. Any tool on the market that doesn't rip the fly apart should be a benefit.

Another tip that can extend the life of your flies is pinching the barb down on the hook. Flies come out of a trout's mouth much more easily.

Helpful Hints

Remember to keep it simple. When buying or selecting flies, don't get overwhelmed. Ask for help and follow the guidelines you've been given. Keep it simple and use proven patterns.

When you store flies, keep them dry. If the hackle gets mashed down, hold the fly over a steam kettle and the hackle will return to its normal shape.

PRODUCTIVE PATTERNS FOR LARGE TROUT

Terminator

Mossback

Double Bunny

Black Ghost

L. L. Crawdad

Beadhead Leech

Beadhead
Woolly Bugger

Rubber Legged
Woven Bugger

Woven Stone Nymph

Improved Grizzly Shrimp

Teeny Egg Sucking Leech
(black)

Teeny Egg Sucking Leech
(ginger)

Teeny Leech
(insect green)

Teeny Leech (natural)

Teeny Sparkle Nymph

Teeny Nymph

Equipment

Chapter 19

Fly Rods

The fly rod is your most important piece of equipment. The reason: the rod casts line and delivers the leader and fly. Fly rods come in a variety of sizes and prices. The material a rod is made from determines its casting ability, price, and weight. Today's fly rods are made of graphite, fiberglass, and bamboo. The following factors should be considered when purchasing a fly rod.

The action of the fly rod is determined by two characteristics: first, how and where the rod bends when casting a line (this is called loading), second, how the rod recovers from the bend in casting the fly line (this is called recovery). A fast-action rod usually bends the upper 30 percent of the rod and creates faster line speed which is appropriate for windy conditions and smaller flies. A medium-action rod usually bends the upper 60 percent of the rod; this is a common action for beginning anglers, or if you fish big flies. The slow action rod usually bends 90 percent of the rod. A slow-action rod is better for setting the hook because it is more forgiving of mistakes.

The length of a fly rod will vary, depending on the fishing technique. The average length is 9 feet. A longer rod, usually 9 1/2 or 10, feet is better for nymphing or float tubing. A longer rod provides better control of the fly line and cast.

The weight of the fly rod is not to be confused with the weight of the line. A six-weight fly rod uses a six-weight fly line. The most common sizes of fly rods range from five-weight to seven-weight. Fly rods from zero- to five-weight are for delicate types of fishing using midges or small dry flies. A six-weight is the most common. Seven- to ten-weight fly rods are designed to cast bigger flies, and for casting in windy conditions. Fly rods range from zero to fifteen in line weight.

Grips

There are as many grip styles as there are different rods. The most popular grips are cigar, half-wells, or full-wells. The best advice is to select a grip that fits your hand and is comfortable when you cast.

After you have purchased your rod, take good care of it. Store your fly rod in an aluminum container or PVC pipe. Clean your rod with a light soap and water solution after heavy use. An abused rod can ruin your day.

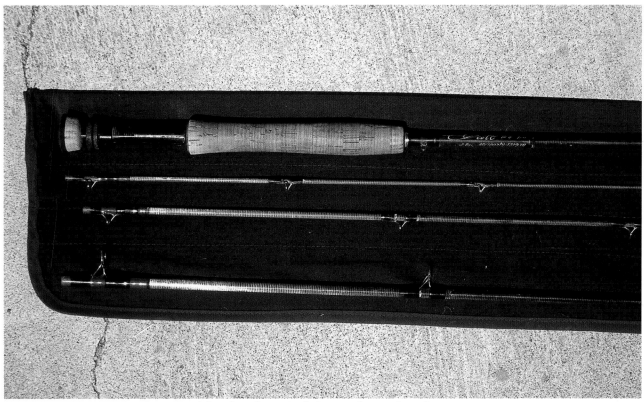

Most fly rods are made in two, three or four pieces.

Chapter 20

Fly Reels

Today's fly reels perform a variety of important functions. The fly reel is a critical piece of equipment for fighting trout. When you select a fly reel here are some important points to remember:

The drag is critical. A smooth, adjustable drag will help slow down a racing trout. The bigger the trout the more important the drag becomes. The two most common types of drag are ratchet-pawl and disc-style. The ratchet-pawl drag is simple and has an adjustable spring which keeps the pawl pressed against the ratchet, making a clicking sound.

The disc-drag style performs like disc brakes on a car, using the smooth friction of one surface against another. The disc-drag style is better for fighting bigger trout.

Fly reels are made of aluminum or graphite and come in a variety of sizes and prices. Aluminum reels intended for saltwater use are anodized for corrosion resistance. Graphite reels are generally less expensive and lack durability.

Different Types

There are three types of action in fly reels: single action, multiplying, and automatic. The reel's action describes the rate at which the fly line is retrieved onto the spool.

Single-action reels have fewer moving parts, are durable, and lighter in weight. A multiplying reel has additional gearing that causes the spool to turn more than once for each turn of the handle. Multiplying reels are usually used for saltwater or large freshwater fish.

The automatic fly reel retrieves fly line with the press of a lever. Automatic fly reels have more parts that are subject to breaking, and usually have poor drag systems. Automatic fly reels also have a tendency to snap light tippets.

Most reels have a direct-drive system. This means the handle rotates with the spool in either direction. Anti-reverse reels have a clutch system, which keeps the handle from spinning backwards.

The size and capacity of a reel determines the type of fish you go after. The bigger the fish, the more capacity you will need for backing material.

There are many different styles of fly reels on the market.

Chapter 21

Fly Leaders and Tippets

The leader creates an invisible connection between the fly line and the fly. It also transfers the energy of the cast smoothly and efficiently, and also helps to give the fly action in the water. When selecting different leaders, there are several important points to consider.

Types of Material

Today's leaders come in a variety of man-made materials, and require far less care Then they used to. They are available in a wide range of diameters, strengths, colors, and hardness. The two most popular types are nylon monofilament and fluorocarbon.

Nylon monofilament is the most common leader material. Monofilament material is inexpensive, durable, has good knot strength, and is nearly invisible. The monofilament does break down quickly in sunlight, and will absorb water causing it to weaken in strength.

Fluorocarbon (polyvinylidene fluoride) leader material is less visible in the water than nylon. The reason is the leader's refractive properties, or the way it bends light rays, more closely matches the properties of water. It has 50 percent more abrasion resistance than nylon, but 50 percent less stretch, requiring a gentle hook set to prevent break off with light tippets. Fluorocarbon material does not absorb water and sunlight does not affect it. The problems with fluorocarbon material are its expense and weaker knot strength.

Parts of a Leader

Leaders are divided into three sections. The butt section makes up about 30 percent of the length, the tapered section makes up about 50 percent, and the tippet section makes up about 20 percent.

The strength of your leader usually will determine your success.

Most leaders taper from a relativity thick butt section to a fine tippet. As a result the leader turns over and presents the fly more delicately. There are two types of tapered leaders: knotted and knotless. A knotted leader is made up of sections of different diameter material, tied end to end. Most people who use knotted leaders build their own leaders.

Knotless leaders taper gradually and may be a better choice for beginners. These leaders work well. The knotless leaders turn over well and are easy to use. The disadvantage is the angler needs to add tippet material to the leader because after numerous fly changes, the leader will be much shorter.

Another choice is tippet spools. When the original leader loses its tapered section, you just add a section of tippet, usually about 12 to 18 inches in length. This way you can continue using the heavy part of the original leader and just change tippet when necessary.

Length

The length of your leader depends on the type of fly-fishing you do. When fishing dry flies, always use the longest leader you can comfortably cast, usually about seven to twelve feet. For nymph fishing shorten your leaders to five to nine feet.

Diameter

Diameters vary from a gossamer .003 to .025, or even larger in large fish applications. The breaking strengths are approximate and slightly on the positive side. The X rating system is widely used in describing leader material. This helps relate the X system to measured diameter. The chart is based on general breaking strengths of tippet material.

Fighting trout in heavy cover requires strong leaders.

Diameter	Rating	Breaking Strength	Fly Size
.011	0X	12 lbs	2-3/0
.010	1X	10 lbs	4-8
.009	2X	9 lbs	6-10
.008	3X	7 lbs	10-14
.007	4X	5 lbs	12-16
.006	5X	4 lbs	14-18
.005	6X	3 lbs	16-22
.004	7X	2 lbs	18-24
.003	8X	1.2 lbs	22-28

The question becomes how true the labeled diameters on the package are. They could be a lot better. There is a big difference between brands. In smaller diameters this becomes more critical.

The size of the tippet correlates with the size of the fly. A common formula to use is: divide the hook size by 3 to get the correct tippet size.

Care

Leader wallets protect leaders and tippet material from sunlight. Always label your leader sleeves for easy identification. Replace your leader or tippet section if it develops a wind knot or wrinkle. A wind knot can reduce line strength by as much as 50 percent.

Brown trout are commonly found in heavy brush.

Chapter 22

Knots

Strong knots are important, weak knots lose fish. Knots should be strong, not bulky, and should do the job effectively. No knot is the best. If you have several people using the same monofilament and tying the same knot, you will find a difference in knot strength among them. Some monofilament does not work well with certain knots.

Most monofilament knots draw down better if you wet them, either with water or saliva. The most important thing to understand about knots is they never break until they begin to slip. It's important to make sure your knots are slip-proof. Always test your knot after you have drawn the monofilament together.

If you have been using a certain knot and want to test its strength use this method: Take two identical hooks; use the new knot on one hook and then attach the other end of the line with a hook using your favorite knot. With two pairs of pliers, grasp the two hooks and pull them apart slowly. Repeat the test by popping them apart quickly. Try both tests several times.

Having the right fly line prepares the angler for a variety of situations.

ARBOR KNOT

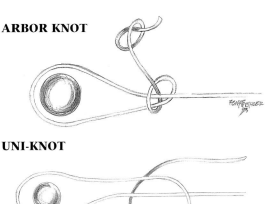

UNI-KNOT

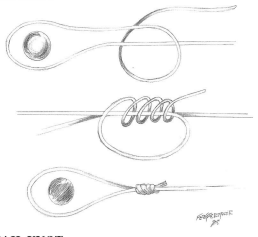

NAIL KNOT

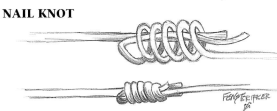

Backing to Reel

There are many ways to make this attachment. The best knot to use is the UNI-Knot. It's strong, easy to tie, and tightens around the reel spool. The UNI-Knot may be the best all-around knot for fishing. You can attach leaders to fly lines, make tapered leaders, and tie on your fly with it.

Backing to Fly Line

Besides the UNI-Knot, one of the best-known knots for attaching the backing to the fly line is the nail knot. The only problem with both of these knots is they can hang up on the guides of your fly rod.

Leader to Fly Line

The nail knot is the most commonly used knot for tying the leader butt to the fly line. The nail knot can be difficult. Most anglers use some type of tool or a tiny section of a hollow tube.

My favorite method to connect the leader to the fly line is a loop-to-loop connection. Each loop is created by using the surgeon's loop knot. This allows me to change leaders fairly regularly. The problem with this type of system is the loop-to-loop connection can catch in the rod guides or pick up vegetation in the water.

Segments of a Leader

The blood knot is the most commonly used knot to build tapered leaders. It's a strong knot, but can be difficult to tie. The double surgeon's knot is a strong knot and, is much easier to tie. An important point to remember about the double surgeon's knot is to draw down tightly on all four tags. A great advantage of the double surgeon's knot is its ability to connect monofilament sections of great difference in diameter, for example 6X tippet to a 3X tippet.

Tippet to Fly

The improved clinch knot is the most popular knot. Other great knots to consider are the UNI-Knot, Trilene knot, and clinch knot. If you want create a loop in front of streamers or nymphs to maintain a more natural action, the UNI-Knot works well. The knot's only problem is that the loop closes after fighting a big trout; therefore you have to retie after each trout.

There are a variety of ways to assemble your equipment, but these are the most common ways to attach all the parts together.

BLOOD KNOT

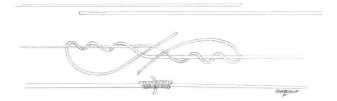

DOUBLE SURGEON'S LOOP

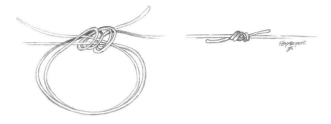

CLINCH KNOT

Monster trout will test any weaknesses in your leader.

Chapter 23

Fly Lines

One of the most confusing items to purchase is your fly line. The fly line delivers the leader and flies to the trout. The weight of the fly line is used to carry the leader and fly to the feeding trout. The rod and line must be compatible. The system for designating lines and rods is called weight. The larger the number is on the rod, the heavier the rod and line. Most rods have a weight rating printed above the grip; for example: 5-6 wt. This means the rod will properly cast either a five- or six-weight fly line. A 5-weight rod will cast a 6- or even 7-weight line without a problem. In most cases, you want to stay fairly close to the recommended size of fly line. The most common fly rod and fly line for trout are a 5- or 6-weight.

Fly lines are made with two basic components; the inner core and the outer core coating. The core is responsible for the strength, stretch, and flexibility of the line. The outer core determines everything else: color, durability, ease of casting, floating, and sinking.

Floating Lines

A floating line does just that, it floats. This line is primarily used for dry flies and midges. Floating lines are the line of choice for casting dry flies on the surface. The fly line is treated with water-resistant agents and air bubbles are added to the coating so the line floats. The line should be cleaned a few times a year to remove dirt, moss, or any other debris.

Taper

The change in diameter of a fly line is called the taper. Some lines have no taper. These lines are called level lines (LL). Level lines are difficult to cast and have limited use. The tapered line loads in the rod and thus enables the cast. The taper of the line is critical to the cast.

Double Taper (DT)

Double-tapered lines are tapered so the diameter gradually increases, like a whip, then remains the same for a specific distance (this section is called the belly), then decreases at the same rate as the other end. The line is tapered exactly the same at the fore and aft. The two advantages to a double taper are: you can swap ends by replacing the worn section with the other end that attaches to the backing, and the double-tapered line can make very delicate casts.

Weight Forward (WF)

The weight-forward line has the weight of the line located in the "head" near the leader. It doesn't take much movement of the rod tip to shoot line effortlessly through the guides. The belly of the head can be fairly short or long, depending on the casting needs of the angler. The weight-forward line can make longer casts to punch through windy conditions, and is designed to cast larger flies.

Sinking Lines

If you want to fish under the surface, use a sinking line. The sink rate is determined by the material (lead or tungsten) added to the line. Some lines sink slowly:—1.25 inches per second—or very fast:—10 inches per second. However, a full-sinking line has its drawbacks. It's hard to detect a soft strike with a full-sinking line.

Sink-Tip Lines

Only the tip (usually 5 to 25 feet, depending on the purpose) sinks and the remaining line floats. The sink rate is different, depending on whether it's slow or fast-sinking model. The advantage of a sink-tip line is that part of the fly line lowers your fly to the level of the trout and the floating section allows you to observe line movement in the water, which will help detect strikes. The sink tip is a much more versatile line compared to the full-sinking line. Sink-tip lines are also much easier to cast.

Line Color

If you fish in crystal-clear creeks or lakes, you should use low-visibility lines. Line color is significant. Fish can be spooked by fly lines, so drab colors like gray or green are best. If you need to see your line to detect strikes and locate flies in choppy water, bright lines are acceptable.

If you are a beginner, I suggest you try a bright-colored line for two reasons; first, you will be able to watch your line direction as you cast, second, you can watch your line on the water and use it as a strike indicator.

The proper flies and lines, fished at the right depth, equals success.

Chapter 24

Fly-Fishing Accessories

Fly fishing anglers tend to be consumer crazy, and the manufacturers are outdoing themselves to make sure we don't run out of things to buy. I carry a gear bag with additional items that accompanies me on my fishing trips. Here is a fairly accurate list of important tools, gadgets, clothing, rain gear, and waders for anglers.

Standard Fishing Gear

Clippers	For trimming or cutting tippet material
Hemostats/Forceps	For removing flies from fish
Hook File	For sharpening hooks
Knot-Tying Tools	For tying leader onto the fly line
Pliers	For flattening hook barbs or pinching weights
Stream Thermometer	For taking water temperature
Tape Measure	For measuring the size of your fish
Fly Floatant	For treating dry flies, or greasing leaders
Lip Balm	For treating your lips
Flashlight	For finding your way back in the dark
Sunscreen	For preventing sun burn
Polarized Sunglasses	For seeing fish in the water
Camera	For taking pictures
Leader material	For replacing tippets or leaders
Fishing License Holder	For holding your license
Notebook/Pen	For recording your day's events
Strike Indicators	For detecting strikes
Split Shot	For adding weight to your leader
Fly Box	For holding your flies
Zinger	For attaching a variety of tools
Net	For landing your fish
Insect Repellent	For keeping mosquitos away
Water Bottle	For keeping the body hydrated
Seine	For collecting insects
Fishing Vests or Waist Pack	For holding all your personal gear
Hat	For keeping the sun off your face
Rain gear	For rainy days
Wading Jacket	For wading in bad weather
Gloves	For keeping your hands warm even if they get wet
Comfortable Clothing	Clothing that blends in with the surroundings

Having good practical equipment will pay off when catching the trout of a lifetime.

Wading Gear

Breathable Waders	For cold-weather wading, or float tubing
Supplex Materials	For wading in hot conditions
Wading Belt	For use with chest waders
Gravel Guards	For preventing sand and gravel from getting into your wading boots
Wader Bag	For storing your waders before and after fishing

Clothing

Like your fishing equipment, clothing should be considered important. You want to ensure a pleasurable fishing experience. If you're going to spend a large amount of money for the very best equipment and waders, you need to wear the correct clothing underneath. Then the next step is to layer properly with the right kind of fabric.

To be comfortable while you're fishing it's important to wear the right combination of fabrics and layers. The whole point to understand layering is for your garments to move perspiration to your outer garments where it can be passed to the outside. This concept is called breathability. As perspiration is passed to the surface it is spread across the surface and evaporated. The most successful material stretches in at least four directions for better freedom of movement. I believe that clothing should be worn in three layers.

The skin layer, this is your underwear. This fabric must wick moisture away from the body quickly. The new lightweight garments made from synthetic materials are best. Look for material that will wick moisture, be comfortable,

A well-equipped fly vest ensures the angler is ready for a variety of situations.

wash easy, and dry quickly. The best fiber is hydrophyllic. Several companies, such as Simms and Patagonia, have the best garments. Polypropylene was an effective layering material but now has been surpassed by hydrophyllic fibers. Silk used to be one of the best, but in all my experiences it does not wick moisture away from the body when it gets wet.

The next layer is the thermal layer. This layer is dependent upon your weather conditions. Remember, light weight for cool days, mid-weight for cold and wet days, and heavy weight for extreme cold and wet days. The heavier the material the warmer it will be. I have found fleece to be the best second layer material. Fleece can be regulated by the thickness of the material. I prefer Windstopper wool clothing from Cabela's. The Windstopper wool garments are very comfortable and they keep the wind and cold from penetrating. Wool materials get heavier when wet but retain their warmth. The combination of wool and windstopper is an unbelievable combination.

The last layer is the outer shell. This layer must protect you from wind, rain, and cold. This material should be windproof, breathable, abrasion resistant, and waterproof. Purchase the best you can afford. Do not cheat yourself with a substitute material, you will be sorry. Look for jackets that are breathable and made of Gore-Tex. Don't purchase water-resistant jackets or any other type of material. Stick with Gore-Tex.

For all fishing conditions, especially the extreme conditions you need to stay comfortable. I've seen anglers struggle the most on hot windy days, rather than extremely cold and wet days. Even on hot days you will be more comfortable by using a good layering system.

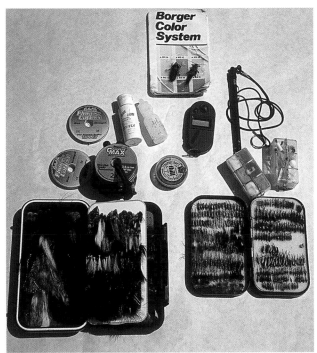

The basic essentials should never be overlooked.

Chapter 25

Float Tubes

As the interest in lake fishing has increased, fly fisher-men are turning to float tubes. Float tubes have increased in popularity because they get anglers closer to trout. Float tubes are the most inexpensive means of gaining mobility on the water. The portability of float tubes is another reason for their popularity. They're light, easy to carry, and allow for quick access to trout. Water that is too deep to wade is now accessible by a float tube. The float tube also gives the fisherman an up-close look at aquatic insects, hatches, feeding patterns and feeding lies for trout. In this section, we are going to examine the basics of float tubes: types, safety, accessories, entering and exiting the water, and care and maintenance.

Different Types

There are many different types of float tubes. All float tubes are considered a Type I personal boat. Float tubes come in various shapes: round, tapered oval, and the U-shape boat (U-shape tubes have a bar on the front that is rotated out of the way for entry into the tube). The polyurethane air bladders replace the old truck-style tubes, and have reduced the weight of the average float tube. Most companies offer two sizes of float tubes: the sixteen-inch inter-tube or the twenty-inch inter-tube.

Over the past several years, companies have been offering innovations such as: back rest, storage pockets, and a quick-release crotch strap. I prefer a float tube with storage pockets for storing rain gear, lunch, fly boxes, etc. The back rest is a comfortable feature to have on your float tube. Float tubes run anywhere from $70 to $200. When shopping for a float tube, pay close attention to: stitching on the shell, zipper location, and safety straps. Look for a double or triple stitch on the seams and a heavy-duty zipper.

You propel through water either by fins or paddles. Most anglers use fins because of their great thrust power. There are two kinds of fins used: Step-in fins and Force Fins. Step-in fins are designed to be worn with wading boots; Force Fins are worn directly over your stocking-foot

Jim Teeny releases a beautiful rainbow trout caught while float tubing.

waders. The fins may sink or float. An extra strap is available to prevent accidental loss of your fins. Force Fins provide great mobility, and you can cover water quickly. The drawback to Force Fins is that you have to paddle backwards and they are difficult to walk in, especially when entering and exciting the water. Step-In Fins strap on to your heels and are designed to streamline against your ankle on the forward stroke, then swing out and dig in on the back stoke. Step-In Fins are easier to walk in in and out of the water.

Safety

Safety should always be your first concern, around any type of water. The float tube was designed for slow-moving water, using a float tube in moving water can be very dangerous. Because your legs and feet are below the tube, there is the risk of your fins or paddles becoming snagged. It's important that you apply a common-sense approach and "wade with your head." When entering the water always look for hazards that could trip you or knock you off balance. Make sure your seat strap is adjusted properly. Never buy a float tube that does not contain a seat strap. Wear clothes that are brighter in color so other boats will see you. Do not tube at night because hazards are harder to see and shallow areas are hard to find. Always go float tubing with someone else. Always wear a flotation device while in your belly boat. The greatest cause of float tubes tipping is over-inflation. A float tube that rides high on the water is at a higher risk of tipping than a float tube that rides lower in the water. Take time to rest. You should frequently visit shore to avoid cramps, chilling, or even hypothermia in severe cases. You should wear chest-high neoprene waders in your tube. Remember that float tubing was designed for still waters.

Accessories

Float tubes have many functional accessories that should be considered when you purchase your tube. All items should be strapped in, there is nothing more disappointing than watching your polarized glasses disappear into the depths of a lake. I place all items in zip-lock storage bags before putting them in the storage pockets. Most float tubes have a rear storage pocket, that can be used as a back rest or splash guard. You need to purchase chest-high neoprene waders, a wader belt, fins, a personal flotation device, and it is always nice to have a rain jacket. Look for waders that have a high back. A wading belt will prevent the waders from riding down while you're seated in the boat. Force fins seem to be the most popular among tubers. Make sure you purchase fin savers. Fin savers are straps designed to hold onto your fins. The last item to mention is a stripping apron, most float tubes have aprons, make sure you don't purchase a float tube without one.

Entering and Exiting

For the beginner, the most difficult part of float tubing is entering and exiting from the water. Let me share with you a procedure that will help you. First scout an area that has

Donna Teeny releases a rainbow trout safely back into the water.

easy access to the water. Avoid areas with heavy vegetation, broken limbs, or any obstacles lying around. Select a hard bottom, mud is a hazard when entering the water.

Once you have determined a good area, carry your fly rod, float tube, and flippers as close to the water as possible. Then unfasten the stripping apron and fold it back. Sit on the tube, put on your fins, and attach the fin savers. Then unsnap the seat strap. Step carefully into the tube, grasp the tube straps and lift the tube up to your waist. Attach the fly rod to the float tube and fasten the rod down. Looking back over your shoulder, slowly begin backing into the water. At this point fasten your seat strap and slowly sit in the water and paddle away. Don't jump into the water wearing a float tube. When paddling, wave your legs around leisurely. After a long day of floating it is much easier to kick swim than propel the water.

When exiting the water follow the same procedure backwards. Remember your legs are going to be tired and fatigued, take your time.

Care and Maintenance

As for care and maintenance of your float tube, before storage, wash it and allow it to dry completely before deflating. Store your tube in a cool, dry place. Make sure you don't fold the tube too tight. When storing your float tube it's best to partially deflate the tube. One problem that can occur is over-inflating the tube, added with a hot day and you can bust the seams on the cover.

Lake fishing from a float tube can be an enjoyable and rewarding experience. Fine tuning your float-tubing tactics will help you enjoy great success. The float tube has added a new dimension to lake fishing. Try it, you might get hooked.

Chapter 26

Pontoon Boats

Pontoon boats have increased in popularity due to their versatility. Pontoon boats can travel farther, faster, and with better mobility than conventional float tubes. They have been designed so fishermen can cast more easily and fish very comfortably. The kick boat has become a personalized water craft. If you match the water craft to your needs and the waters you fish, you can enjoy many spectacular days of fishing.

Different Types

There are four different categories of pontoon boats. The following are general guidelines that will help you decide which pontoon boat is best for your needs. I have included float tubes and U-boats in this chapter.

Type I

Pontoon boats, including all float tubes, U-boats, and smaller pontoon boats belong in this category. These types of boats are used for stillwater fishing. They are low-profile boats. A low-profile boat is not as affected by wind because it rides so low in the water. Type I boats are compact, slow to maneuver, light weight, and affordable. These boats usually have small storage spaces. Some of the smaller pontoon boats have rowing frames and when combined with the use of fins, can move very quickly.

Type II

Slow water craft include pontoon and raft-style kick boats with pontoons smaller than 7 feet long and 14-inch diameter tubes. You can sit above the water and carry some gear with these boats. Type II boats are best used for ponds, lakes,

Using a durable water craft can provide many lasting memories.

and some Class I rivers, if they do not have any hazards, major obstructions, or require technical maneuvering. These boats are generally twice as faster as type I boats. Many type II boats have rowing frames, but be sure to purchase one with a foot rest. Do not use an anchor on these boats when in moving water, you can capsize. Curve-bottom boats are better at maneuvering than flat-bottom boats. Most models deflate and pack up into a compact package.

Type III

Fast-water craft: these boats have a rocker hull shaped much like a banana. They can be used on lakes, Class I rivers, and some Class II rivers. The better the boater, the more versatility the craft will have. Some experienced anglers can use these boats on Class III rivers, if they have experience. Type III boats are usually the choice of advanced fishermen. The pontoons are longer than 7 feet and have a diameter of 14-plus inches. Type III boats are more mobile than a drift boat or raft. The rocker-style pontoon aids in maneuvering and are safer than smaller boats. Check to make sure the rowing system is heavy duty, the oars are made of a sturdy material, and that the boat has a strong foot brace. Most anglers use fins as their main source of propulsion. The oars are rigged and ready at a moments notice.

Type III boats can hold from 300 to 500 pounds. The boats usually contain large areas for storage. The more weight you carry, the deeper the boat rides, and the frames must be adjusted to compensate for the weight. The boats usually contain an anchor system. Use your anchor in slow or shallow water, but never in fast water. Always have a knife handy in case you need to cut the rope. Type III boats have several disadvantages: they are affected by the wind, they are more expensive, and they are much heavier than other personal craft.

Type IV

Type IV boats are cargo pontoon boats. They are designed for long river trips, or just carrying a lot of equipment. The pontoons are usually at least ten feet long and the tube diameter is 18 inches or more. Most of these boats are designed for rowing. You will ride high on the water with these boats. Type IV boats are best for Class I, Class II, and Class III rivers. Because of their construction, they are very heavy. Type IV boats are also the most expensive. Some Type IV boats have air bladders to increase safety. Type IV boats have very sturdy platforms to rest cargo, equipment, or even stand on.

Accessories

Fins are the most common way of maneuvering in water. With practice your fins will propel you in any direction with ease. If you plan to fish for a long time, use lightweight fins. Long fins do not work well in shallow areas. Short wide fins are much better in rivers, and are much easier to walk in. When I am fishing in a river I stand up in the shallows and use the boat for stability.

If you have the option of oars, get them. Oars are best for rowing long distances or in technical water. When you purchase oars make sure the oar blades float. If you should happen to drop them, the oar blades won't sink or get tangled with your feet.

Oarlocks should be clamped on, do not buy oarlocks that are pinned in. You need to be able to move your oars quickly. Oarlock post holes should be angled to the outside, not completely vertical. The U-shaped oar locks should be pinned. Rubber stoppers on the oars help them stay in place.

Anchoring in moving water is very tricky. An anchor that is too light can cause trouble. I believe a good weight is 10 pounds or more. Always anchor in shallow or still water, this way you can retrieve the anchor with ease. It is important to carry a knife for rope cutting. If you should need the knife, you don't want to spend time looking for it. I carry a razor-blade knife on my life vest. If needed, I can reach up for it then cut the rope in seconds.

Maneuvering

Start by launching your pontoon boat into a couple of feet of water, then angle it parallel to the shore and begin scissor kicking. If you don't go straight, angle your fins accordingly and try again. As you turn left and right, angle your fins in the proper position. Next, stop and rotate one fin in a circle, this is called a spin. Practice in both directions. Master this phase before going on.

Getting used to the oars takes practice. Learn to row backwards and forwards. If you want to turn, pull on one oar depending on which direction you want to travel. In a river, a missed oar stroke or fin movement can place you in danger quickly. Practice, practice, practice before you try moving water! Unskilled fishermen using improper equipment are at much higher risk than fishermen that practice. Know your limits and choose the proper pontoon boat for your needs and skills.

Fishing from a pontoon boat can be one of the most rewarding experiences in fishing. Over the years, I have enjoyed the personal craft that guides me to more remote fishing areas. You will be amazed at how effective you will become after mastering the pontoon boat.

Jim Teeny releases an unsuspecting rainbow trout.

Section E
Fishing Techniques

Chapter 27

Casting

The fundamentals of casting discussed in this chapter represent the common skills of all good casters. If all of the following casting fundamentals are properly executed, you will perform better. Fly-casting differs from other methods of casting. Because the fly weighs so little, you cast the weight of the fly line, not the weight of the object at the end of your line. Here are the most important fundamentals of fly casting:

• Learn the terminology of casting.
• Line speed is important in casting your line.
• There must be a pause at the end of each stroke. The weight of the fly line which bends the rod is called loading. Because the line must be straight, for the rod to load, you should pause, and then allow the line to straighten.
• Slack line during the casting stroke should be minimal. Eliminating the slack during the casting stroke will allow the rod to load properly.
• As you cast, keep the rod tip in a straight line. The rod tip must stay in the same horizontal and vertical planes. Increased acceleration will help the flow of the line stay on the same plane.
• In most casting situations, a tight loop is usually best because a tight loop has little wind resistance and better accuracy.
• There is an important relationship between the casting arc size and the amount of bend in the fly rod. A short line is made by a short stroke; a long line is made by a long stroke.
• Dropping your wrist too far on the back cast opens the loop.
• Power must be applied at the proper time of the stroke.
• Practice, practice, practice.

Every fly fisherman should know the following casts: You should know the overhead cast, false cast, roll cast, shooting line, and the double haul. Each cast will increase your odds of catching trout in different situations.

Overhead Cast

The overhead cast is used to pick up line and lay it back down in order to change your target, or cast to your target. Use an overhead cast for short to middle distance targets.

False Cast

The false cast begins the same as the overhead cast. The difference is the overhead cast allows the line to settle on the water. The false cast is a continuous motion. Timing is the most important part of false casting. The acceleration, speed, and stop are the important phases of false casting.

Stance

Place your feet comfortably apart. If you're right handed, place your left foot slightly forward, if you're left handed do the reverse. Place your thumb on top of the rod handle, and grip with your wrist and forearm pointed in a straight line.

Power Phase

Point the rod tip down, then bring the rod backward, raising your forearm smoothly, keeping your wrist and forearm in a straight line. The gradual movement of speed helps you begin to focus the energy of the cast toward your target. The rod tip should move straight back.

BACK CAST

The back cast starts the flow of energy in casting.

FORWARD CASTING MOTION

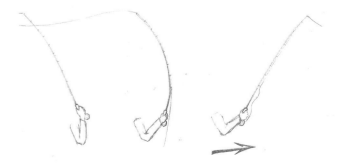

As you cast, keep the rod tip in a straight line.

Pause Phase

As the rod tip nears vertical, stop your arm, allowing the rod to load the line. Even with poor acceleration and speed, stopping the rod will form a tight loop and cause the line to roll properly. When the line has straightened, begin with the forward stroke. Push your arm smoothly toward the target. Stop the rod when it reaches the 45-degree angle. Snap your wrist forward creating the forward loop. Lower the rod slowly towards your target so the line will drop softly on the water.

Casting Plane

The path of the rod tip and line should travel through the air in a straight line. This is called the casting plane. Keep your casting plane level to make sure your rod tip follows the same path. As you cast, keep the rod tip in a straight line. The rod tip must stay on the same horizontal and vertical planes. Gradual acceleration ensures that the line will flow out straight, on the same plane. If there are trees or brush behind you, tilt the casting plane forward to raise the back cast. Lowering your casting plane with a sidearm cast can help you avoid overhanging brush and is more effective in a head wind. Whichever plane you cast in, keep the path of the rod tip in a straight line.

Roll Cast

The roll cast allows you to cast line forward without a back cast. The key is to load the rod by using the friction of the water on the line. Lift your rod tip slowly until the line is about a foot behind your rod and the rest of the line is on the water in front of you. When the line stops

Casting across a large body of water requires the proper skills and technique.

momentarily, this pause allows the water to grip the line creating friction as you begin to load the rod with the line. Accelerate steadily, making a snap with the rod, creating a short speed stroke. Let the fly line roll out in front of you. The fly line should form a loop and then straighten out before settling on the water.

Shooting Line

This method involves making several false casts, then letting out the desired amount of line to reach your target. Lengthening your casting arc gives you extra momentum required for long casts. Stopping the rod tip farther on the back cast, and aiming your forward cast higher, creates a larger arc. Long casts (50 feet or more) require an even longer casting arc. The rod, at times, will be nearly parallel to the water at the end of the back cast.

Double Haul

The formula for distance casting is Mass x Velocity. In fly-casting, mass is the weight of the fly line. The more bend in the rod, the faster the rod will load and unload which will generate more line velocity.

To double haul, make a smooth short downward haul, about 4 to 6 inches, during the acceleration phase of the back cast. Bring your line hand back up immediately after you haul. Let the line unroll behind you as on a normal cast. Then, make a second haul, equal in length to the first, during the acceleration phase of the front cast. Finally, bring your line hand up again immediately after the haul.

Casting requires timing and an equal amount of energy on each phase of the cast.

Chapter 28

Fishing Tactics

Nymph fishing is the most consistent and productive method of taking trout with flies. Whether it's a stream or lake, cold or warm, nymphs are always available in the water.

Nymphs imitate the natural nymph, larvae, or pupae, and even other aquatic foods. Nymphs can be weighted or not weighted. They can vary in materials used to tie them and in size.

Detecting strikes is the hardest part of nymph fishing. There are many different nymph fishing techniques. The best solution is to use a strike indicator while your nymph fishing. If you feel a pause in the line, set the hook. The following are the most common ways to fish with nymphs.

Strike Indicators

There are many different strike indicators available on the market today, from cork, yarn, float putty, and twist ons. Indicators are used to detect strikes; much like a bobber is used when worm fishing. Position the indicator up the leader approximately twice the depth of the water. In slower currents, place the indicator up the leader just above the depth of the water. In faster currents, place the indicator a least three times the depth of the water.

Different Types of Weights

There are several types of weight you can use on your leader: lead or lead-substitute split shot, twist-on lead and molded tungsten compound. The purpose of weight is to get your nymph down to the level at which the trout are feeding. Attach your weight to the leader or just above the tippet knot. Use enough weight to carry your fly to the right level. You can attach several split shot to make adjustments in depth.

A cutthroat trout caught by drifting the fly at the correct depth.

Jim and Donna Teeny complete a double using different tactics.

Multiple Flies

When you add another fly to your system, it's called a dropper. An additional fly can be added in a variety of ways. Remember to tie a dropper fly to at least a 12-inch piece of tippet material that is lighter than the leader material. You can tie your extra fly on by adding another piece of tippet to the hook bend of the main fly, or by using the tail end of your knot material where you added on your tippet.

Casting Tactics

When casting shot and strike indicator setups, the normal casting stroke, tight loops, and false casting won't work. It requires a different cast. Casts should be shorter, ranging from 10 to 30 feet. Two casts that work very well in this situation are the open loop cast and the lob cast. Because of the extra weight added to the fly line, both of these casts will eliminate many of the problems.

There are several strategies you should practice when nymph fishing. The shorter the cast, the more line control and drift of your nymph you will have. Follow the drift of the indicator with your rod tip. Continue to mend the line as the indicator drifts through the water. As you pick up slack because of the indicator getting closer, draw in slack with your line hand and raise your rod tip higher. To continue a long drift with the nymph, lower your rod tip as the nymph passes you. Establish a pattern of casting much like shooting a shotgun. Work the water in front of and farther away from you.

Chapter 29

Different Methods

There are many different methods of retrieving your fly to catch trout. In this section I will briefly discuss the methods that are successful. You will find many variations of each method. It's important that you are able to perform different methods for different situations.

The Sawyer Method

Frank Sawyer from England pioneered this method over fifty years ago. The whole concept behind the Sawyer method is to cast a nymph directly above a feeding trout, inducing a strike. The key to catching trout using the Sawyer method is to read the speed of the current and to know how quickly your nymph sinks. The Sawyer method is a good technique to use on clear bodies of water were you can see the trout rising. You must also be able to place a fly within inches of a trout, with no drag. This method can be used with mayflics, caddisflies, nymphs, terrestrials and emergers.

To perform the Sawyer method, cast upstream far enough for the fly to reach the level the trout are at. Then watch for any type of strike. Keep your fly rod tip low, so you don't spook the trout. Use a sidearm cast to keep the glare of the rod out of the trouts' vision.

Position yourself downstream and across current from the rising trout. Cast far enough upstream of the rising trout, so the nymph has time to sink to the trout's level. Try to use a sidearm cast when casting during these difficult situations.

The strip/tease technique is a very deadly technique.

Follow the drift of the fly with your rod tip. Watch the trout for a sign it has taken the fly. You may have to try this technique many times to get the trout to take the fly.

The Brooks Method

The Brooks method was designed by Charles Brook. It was designed to drift big, weighted flies to large trout in swift water, and is the most commonly used method. This method is designed to fish with a dead-drift technique. The Brooks method requires heavier rods and tippets for lifting big trout out of deep water. You should use a short leader with enough weight to sink your fly to the bottom. This method can be used with mayflies, caddisflies, nymphs, streamers, terrestrials, and emergers.

The Brooks method requires you to cast upstream far enough to get your fly to the bottom of the river, usually about fifteen feet. Aim the rod tip above the point where the leader enters the water, this allows the fly to sink. Lift the rod tip to take control of any slack in the line; this is also called high sticking. The farther the cast the higher the rod tip. Follow your fly as the line swings directly downstream to you. You must be able to constantly mend your line as the fly drifts in the swift water. Keep your cast within 20 feet. Use a lob cast to reset the cast technique again.

The Brooks Method is best when you find places where the fast current drops off into a deep riffle of boulders with a fast current.

The Leisenring Lift

When done properly, the Leisenring lift can be one of the deadliest techniques for nymphs and emergers. This technique gives the fly the life-like action of the natural rising to the surface. The current speed and depth of the fly are critical in presentation. Most trout will follow the fly to the surface before taking it. Follow through all the way to the end of the drift. This method can be used with mayflies, caddisflies, nymphs, terrestrials, and emergers.

The technique is as follows; stand across the current and slightly above where the trout is feeding. Allow enough distance for your fly to fall to the level of the trout. Then, follow the drift of the fly with your rod tip just as you did in the Sawyer method. If you need to mend line to keep the fly moving naturally, do so. Next, stop the rod tip as the fly is about a foot from the trout. The fly will begin to rise upward with the current. Lift the rod upward to make a gentle rise with the fly, and set the hook gently.

The Reach Mend

The reach mend is very successful for delivering the fly across currents. As the line moves downstream, lift the rod tip to keep the excess slack off the water. As the line passes you, move the rod tip to your downstream side. This feeds slack into the drift and keeps the fly riding drag free. You can continually mend your line as the fly moves through the water. This method can be used with mayflies, caddisflies, nymphs, streamers, terrestrials, and emergers.

Heave and Leave

Trout in stillwaters cruise about in search of food. The heave and leave technique is just what it says. Sometimes adult flies and emergers move very little on top of the water. The current of the water provides enough movement for the fly. When I perform any of the heave and leave methods I like to use a strike indicator so I can detect any movement of a trout taking the fly. This method can be used with mayflies, caddisflies, nymphs, terrestrials, and emergers.

There are several variations you can apply to the heave and leave method. When you fish dry flies or emergers, cast the fly to a selected spot and then give it tiny twitches. Keep your fly rod tip pointed down so you can remove as much slack in the line as possible. It's important to have an extreme amount of patience. Don't move the fly even an inch or two. I've waited up to five minutes, waiting for a trout to pick the fly up.

Another technique I've found to be successful is to cast the fly to a selected spot, let the fly drift, and every 20 to 30 seconds strip the fly towards you. Strip the fly about three four-inch strips, then let it sit again for 20 to 30 seconds.

Strip/Tease Retrieve

The strip/tease retrieve has many variations depending on the type of motion you want to create with your fly. This is one of my favorite techniques to use with streamers, terrestrials, or any large fly patterns.

This method requires casting to a selected spot, then retrieving the fly in an erratic motion that will entice the trout to bite. Use short strips of four to six inches in length.

Another technique is to cast the fly to a selected spot then strip the fly several inches and pause. While pausing, wiggle your rod tip. Most of the time trout will take the fly when it pauses. It's very important to pay attention during the pause, when you feel the strike, lift your rod tip. If you are fishing lakes or still water, remember to keep your rod tip down, which helps take slack out of your line.

Popping Method

The popping method is used with large stoneflies, streamers, and any type of forage fish patterns. The popping method is a variation of the strip/tease retrieve.

Learning to reach and mend your fly line creates a drag-free drift.

To perform this method, cast towards the bank of a river or lake and pop the fly towards you by using the rod. Then gather the slack in the line and pop the fly towards you. The motion becomes a pop - pause - pop technique. This method will bring big trout out from under the banks of a river.

Hand-Twist Retrieve Method

The hand-twist retrieve is my favorite retrieve to use on still water. This method has produced more big trout than any other method I've used.

To perform the hand-twist retrieve, cast your line to a selected spot, slowly gather line by alternating the forefinger and middle finger and ring finger. Remember, the deeper the water, the slower the retrieve. If there is a fast current associated with the deep water, I will perform a hand-twist retrieve with an occasional line strip. This method works best with a high rod tip, but lowering the rod tip to different levels helps take the slack out of the line. The hand-twist retrieve method is used with large stoneflies, nymphs, emergers, streamers, and forage fish patterns.

Greased Tippet Method

The greased tippet method is best fished with midges, dry flies, and emergers. This method imitates any type of insect that swims, gets caught, or is trapped in the surface film.

To perform the greased tippet method, you treat your leader with floatant up to a few inches from the fly. Put the floatant on your fingers and rub it onto the leader. The leader will float on the surface, holding the fly in the surface film. I also use a small strike indicator on the leader to detect the strike of the trout. This is my favorite method to fish midge pupae.

Chapter 30

The Final Phase

Trout are very delicate fish. A trout out of the water for more than two minutes or more has damaged gills and will usually not survive. Here are some techniques you ought to know about fighting and handling fish to assure they will survive after they have been released.

Strike

There are many different ways to set the hook when a trout strikes your fly. The best procedure is to pull a four-inch tug with your line. Your rod will automatically recoil helping you set the hook. To many times we try to set the hook by raising the rod tip which usually results in missing the fish.

Fighting

Fight the fish from the reel. As soon as you can get the line on the reel, let your drag do its job. Keep your trout on as short a line as possible.

Don't keep the rod tip up. That's right. By keeping the rod tip high, it releases the pressure on the trout. You must take the fight to the fish, not the other way around. When you hook a big fish, it's not what the fish does but what you do that determines the outcome. Different rod positions will exert different amounts of pressure on the fish. A high rod tip (90-degree angle) will exert minimal pressure. A rod tip at 45-degree angle will exert the maximum amount of pressure. If you want to continue the pressure on the trout, angle the rod, so the butt not the tip is flexed.

Landing

Landing trout is critical, because most big trout escape at the time of the strike and during the netting process. When landing a trout by yourself, rotate the reel so it is facing the rear. Hold the line under the finger of your rod

Keeping the trout in water allows for a quick recovery.

hand. Be ready to release the line immediately if the trout makes a run. Net the trout when its head is facing you. When you control the trout's head, you have better success.

Handling

The best way to handle a trout is to not handle it at all. Barbless hooks make the release much easier on the trout. One approach that works very effectively is to turn the trout upside down. Do not squeeze the trout. If your going to take a photo, keep the trout in water. Before touching the trout, wet your hand. Never touch the gills. Release the trout facing into the current. Take the time to revive the trout. Hold a played fish by the tail with one hand and gently support the fish from underneath, remembering to avoid the gills. Move the trout back and forth to help replace the oxygen. Gently moving the trout in the water will help engage more oxygen into the gills. Slightly rubbing the belly can also help revive the trout. Practice on every trout like it was a ten-pound trout. Practice catch and release.

Catch and Release

Fortunately, most trout today are released. Because fishing is such a popular sport, it's obvious that streams could not continue to produce good fishing unless fishermen returned their share of trout back to the water.

There is very little evidence disputing the concept of catch-and-release fishing. It is critically important that fishermen spend time learning how to release trout properly. If catch and release is practiced properly, each trout will have an excellent chance of survival.

Care of Your Trophy

I certainly appreciate a first-class taxidermy job on a big trout, but all things should be kept in moderation. Here are some simple guidelines to follow when preserving your trophy.

The less you handle a trout, the better for safe effective recovery.

Jim Teeny carefully handles a large trout before releasing it back into the water.

Carry a camera and immediately take color pictures of the trout so the taxidermist can capture its true colors. Write down noticeable charachteristics of the trout that catch your eye. Do not field dress the trout. Wipe Borax into the skin of the fish, then wrap cheese cloth or freezer paper around it. Next, wrap a layer of plastic around the trout. Then freeze the trout. Deliver the trout to the taxidermist frozen. Great taxidermists are rare, expensive, and usually very busy. It may take a long time before you receive your mount back. Do not compromise, or settle for cheaper work.

Photographing Your Trophy

There are several techniques for photographing trout. Always remember that the longer the trout is out of the water, the more damage can be done to the trout. Never squeeze a trout, hold it by the gills, drop it, beach it, or keep it out of the water for more than a few seconds at a time.

The best way to hold a small or medium size trout is to cup your hand gently under the belly and lift it just out of the water.

The best way to support a large trout is by holding the tail with one hand. Support its weight by placing your other hand underneath its belly. Keep the fish close to the water, so if it falls it won't land on the ground. Try to take the picture, as the trout is slowly lifted out of the water. It makes for a more lifelike picture with water dripping off the trout.

Section F
Special Situations

Chapter 31

Fishing Seasons

Different patterns, lines, leaders, and presentations—nothing remains the same and can change by the minute, hour, day, week, or season. All fishing waters constantly change because of weather, temperature, barometric pressure and other factors that influence trout and aquatic insects.

Spring

During early spring, lakes and rivers are temperamental due to water temperatures, aquatic insect activity, and the start of plant growth. Spring is one of the toughest times to locate trout. To be successful, you must understand the essentials of water temperature, oxygen, food, and thermal stratification.

During spring, big flies go hand in hand with big trout. The food source is usually the largest of the season, so enjoy. I prefer dark colors on leeches in sizes 4 to 8. Flies to consider are Woolly Buggers, leech patterns, Zonkers, scuds, and big nymphs.

In spring, remember retrieves should be slow. Trout are very slow moving, and you want to keep the fly in front of their nose. Trout are cold blooded and their entire systems slow down in cold water. I find that trout don't chase their food in the spring, they wait for it to come to them.

I prefer to start fishing with a sink-tip or intermediate sinking fly line. Trout are seldom leader shy in the spring. I usually start with a 4X to 3X tippet and work smaller if need be. Trout aren't as picky, so you can spend more time locating them.

Whatever equipment you use, remember spring brings strong cold winds. You must be able to cast 40 to 60 feet into the wind.

The best time to fish is after the sun has appeared on the water. By late afternoon, the day is over. Midday is the quality time. Enjoy sleeping in and spend quality time during the middle of the day.

Summer

The summer is the essence of the sport of fly fishing. Trout are active, there are prolific hatches, calm weather patterns, and lakes and rivers are fishable. To the adventurous

Fly fishing during the spring offers wonderful scenery.

angler, there's a smorgasbord of fishing opportunities. Trout are also more predictable during the summer.

Flies can range in size from 22 to size 8. Start with patterns like the Prince Nymph, Hare's Ear, or Pheasant Tail Nymphs. Many of my flies are determined by the hatch of the day. Start with nymphs and leeches in the morning, and as the day wears on move to emergers and adult patterns.

Use fly rods 9 to 10 feet long and 5- to 7-weight line. In summer, fast-action rods are more successful for throwing a tight loop with delicate presentations.

It is good to have a sink-tip, double tapered, and still-water fly lines on hand. I use different lines throughout the day depending upon the situation. Casting must be a form of art in the summer. Long and accurate casts are the minimum; you must be able to hit your target without hesitation.

I find trout are readily available in feeding lies in rivers and the plant zone in lakes. The best time to locate trout is early morning and late evening; they seem to be the peak feeding periods during the whole summer, except when certain odd events occur.

During the summer you must use a variety of retrieve styles, lines, and flies to imitate the life stages of the insects. Being flexible is the key to success in the summer; what works one day, may not work the next.

Fall

During fall, feeding periods begin to shorten, hatches dwindle, and the feel of winter brings a sense of urgency to trout. Fall also offers the opportunity to fish during the brown trout and brook trout spawn. This is my favorite time of the year.

Fall fishing can produce trout with magnificent colors.

Stay with the same tackle as you used in the summer. Constantly check and recheck leaders for nicks or knots.

Most insects are smaller in the fall, except for terrestrials and leeches. Patterns you used in summer will work in fall, just add a little flash or change the color. Many water drainages are at their lowest of the season, and the water is sparkling clear. I also believe your casts don't have to be as long as in the summer. Trout move into the shallows to feed on minnows and other large food sources. There's no mystery to finding trout in the fall. The best time of day is whenever you get there. Fishing can be very productive in the morning, midday, or evening.

In fall, heavy tippets are the norm, and expect big fish. Weather can change suddenly, so be prepared. Your presentations should be at their best, and I find that some days retrieving quickly is successful, and the next day you can't go slowly enough.

Winter

Fly fishing during winter is a thrilling, ice-cold experience, with many opportunities to refine skills that need adjustment from the summer and fall months. The water is colder, and cold blooded trout move slowly, often they hold in large holes to survive the winter months. Trout often go many days without eating, and only feed when it is absolutely necessary.

Use small nymphs ranging from size 14 to 20. This is a great time for catching trout on midge or pupae patterns. If you are fishing deep, make your retrieves slow. Put the fly on the nose of the trout.

Winter fishing requires extreme patience in ice-cold weather.

Chapter 32

Drift Boat Fishing

During the course of a fishing trip, the guide changes the speed of the boat depending on many different variables. It's important that anglers work together while casting from the boat. I've seen many guided trips become a disappointment for two reasons: First, the anglers don't work together in harmony. Second, the anglers don't cast with accuracy. Remember, practice, practice, practice.

Alternating Casts

As a rule, the angler in the back of the boat (stern) watches the angler in the front (bow). As soon as the angler in the bow casts, the angler in the stern should cast. Wait until the angler in the bow casts again before you cast again. By alternating casts, anglers work together in harmony. Also the angler in the bow casts only to water in front of the boat. The angler in the stern only casts to water in the middle of and behind the boat. Always put the angler who can mend line in the back of the boat.

Teamwork

The boat, current speed, and casting all combine to create challenges. When the boat is moving the same speed as the current, the anglers should make their casts at a 45-degree angle downstream from the midline of the boat. This way the fly floats ahead of the boat. If the boat is moving slower than the current, the anglers should make casts at a 90-degree angle from mid boat, therefore allowing for a longer drift.

It is important to minimize your false casting. You don't have a lot of time to present your fly. As a guide I've always believed that casting is 40 percent of the time and 60 percent of the time you should be mending. When you cast, get the most out of your drift. Mend your line upstream or downstream, depending on the speed of the current and the boat's drift speed.

Fishing from a raft or drift boat provides the opportunity to cover a lot of productive fishing water.

Drift boat fishing allows access to water not heavily fished.

Chapter 33

First Aid

In this section we will deal with some of the most common injuries that occur while fishing. Every person should take a basic first-aid and CPR class. This way we all stay current on procedures in first aid and CPR. The following are only guidelines when administering first aid and CPR, and are not a substitute for taking classes.

Treatment for Shock

- Control any external bleeding
- Lay the person flat on their back
- Elevate legs about 8 - 12 inches, unless you suspect a neck, head or back injury
- Cover the victim according to weather conditions
- Keep the victim calm until help arrives

Bleeding

Bleeding must be controlled to prevent shock. There are two types of blood loss: external and internal.
External Wounds:
Do
- Get help
- Apply direct pressure
- Elevate limb, do not elevate if a fracture is suspected
- Press at arterial pressure point
- Treat for shock according to weather conditions
Do not
- Remove any dressings
- Use a tourniquet
- Overheat
- Give anything by mouth

Drowning

Any time a person is found unresponsive in water do the following:
Do
- Call 911 or get help
- Overview the scene for your safety in attempting a water rescue
- Open the airway and begin rescue breathing in the water
- Begin CPR once a firm, hard surface is reached
- Cover with dry blankets
- Be prepared for the person to vomit
Do not:
- Put yourself in danger trying to make a daring rescue
- Waste time trying to remove water from the person's mouth or lungs
- Give up on a drowned person, continue CPR

Hypothermia

Hypothermia can occur in non-freezing temperatures if certain conditions exist. The big problem with hypothermia is that the victim many times does not realize they are being overcome.

Symptoms include:
- Uncontrolled shivering, pale and cold, slurred speech, motor skill problems, and/or mental confusion.
- Their reasoning ability is being impaired by the cooling process.
Do
- Avoid rough handling
- Remove from cold, get victim to warm area
- Remove wet clothing, cover with dry clothing
- Give warm fluids, if victim is totally conscious
- Be prepared to provide CPR or rescue breathing
Do not
- Give liquids containing alcohol or caffeine
- Rub cold fingers, toes, or other body parts
- Allow frostbitten body part to refreeze
- Stop CPR

Heat Stroke

Heat emergencies fall into three categories: 1) heat cramps, 2) heat exhaustion, 3) heat stroke. Heat stroke is a critical emergency as the victim's body has lost it's ability to cool itself and, if left unchecked, can cause central nervous system damage.
Do
- Call 911 or get help
- Cool victim quickly (wrap wet towels around the body and head, then fan)
- Give small sips of water as long as the victim is fully conscious
Do not
- Give aspirin to victim to try to reduce temperature
- Give salt tablets
- Use ice packs or ice water to cool

Insect Stings
Do
- In case of bee sting: scrape off stinger using credit card, plastic knife, etc. Wash well with soap and water, cover bite with dressing, and apply cold pack. Call 911 or get help.
- In severe allergic reactions caused by other sources: recognize reaction as a 911 call or get help. Do not

hesitate to activate fire or rescue crews. Place in shock position.

Do not
- In case of bee sting: use tweezers to remove the stinger; this will push the toxin from poison sac into the wound.
- Apply tourniquet

Embedded Fish Hook

Do:
- Take a short piece of fish line, and loop it around the shank or bend of the embedded hook. Then grasp the fish line firmly with one hand. With the opposite hand, press down firmly on the eye of the hook. As you press down on the hook, pull quickly with the fish line. Pull the line parallel to the surface of the skin.
- Treat for bleeding

Lightning

Lightning can be one of the deadliest weather events that affects fishing. When you see lightning or hear thunder, take action. A safety slogan everyone should remember is: "If you see it (lightning) - flee it (take shelter); if you can hear it (thunder) - clear it (quit activity). Wait at least 30 minutes after the last lightning strike or sound of thunder before resuming fishing. The following are guidelines for lightning and thunder:
- Plan your escape route in advance.
- Avoid water, high ground, and open spaces. Avoid all metal objects, wires, fences, motors, and machinery.
- Unsafe areas are underneath canopies, and trees. Safe areas include fully enclosed buildings, low ground, clumps of bushes, or metal vehicles. Keep the windows of the vehicle closed. Don't touch any metal parts, and the rubber on the wheels offers no protection.
- To calculate lightning distances use the following formula. If you hear thunder, and the associated flash within your auditory range, it is about 6-8 miles away. The distance from point A to point B can also be 6-8 miles away.
- If you find yourself in a lightning storm and can't flee, do the following: remove all metal objects (including baseball hats) place your feet together, duck your head, and crouch into a baseball catcher's stance with your hands over your ears. Avoid standing next to people (at least fifteen feet).

People who have been struck by lightning, do not carry an electrical charge and are safe to apply first aid. Get emergency help immediately.

The weather in the high country can change very quickly. Plan your escape carefully.

Chapter 34

Safety Tips

The information in this chapter is crucial; it may save your life. It's always the small things that creep up and hurt you badly.

Wading

- Always wear a wading belt with chest waders. Chest and hip waders are extremely dangerous if they fill with water.
- Be careful when wading in water that is waist deep or deeper.
- Stand sideways in swift current to minimize the force of the water and prevent your feet from being swept out from under you.
- Pivot upstream when turning around in fast water. If you pivot downstream, the current pushes you too fast.
- If you fall into the water, put your rod in your teeth and face your legs in front of you - down river. Use your arms to help you push to shore.
- Stand on a plastic sheet or mat when removing your waders. This prevents objects from puncturing the wader material.
- Hang waders upside down in a cool, dark place, using wader hangers.

Boating

- Always boat with another person.
- Always wear a flotation device when on the water.
- Check your boat out prior to putting the boat on the water.
- Don't have any loose straps or loops hanging from the boat, they can get snagged on things.

Jim Teeny releases a monster rainbow after wading through snags and boulders.

Chapter 35

Planning a Fishing Trip

Planning a fishing trip can be an exciting challenge or an agonizing experience. When planning a trip, many questions arise: Where to fish, when to go, what equipment to use, how to choose your guide, and where to stay? As an experienced guide, I'll begin by answering the most asked questions. When you decide where you want to fish, and before you make any plans, use the Internet; contact local fly shops. Most fly shops can accommodate almost anyone with their travel plans. The fly shops can help you with the following; places to fish, private water fishing, motel reservations and possible places to eat.

Hiring a Guide

A good outfitter will recommend the best fishing times, flies, and type of guide you will need. The cost of hiring a guide can range from $100 to $300 dollars per person per day. Lunch is normally included in trip prices, but always asks. It is expensive to hire a guide, but well worth it. A guide can teach you many things about the area's fishing. Most guided trips include one to three people.

Do your research to find a good guide. Your guide must be able to pull you from a bad situation, keep you alive, happy, and successful. Most guides are good at what they do and are proud of their profession. There are things you can do to gain a guide's respect and friendship, things that will make for many enjoyable fishing days together and create a bond that will last a lifetime. Like you, your guide wants to have fun. They want to be treated like a human being. Remember, he or she is your guide, not your slave. The guide has to keep you, the boat, and the equipment out of trouble and in good working order. Guides will be up early in the morning and will not go to bed until late at night. Your guide will work harder for you, if you work with him. Helping your guide will add time to your trip, so ask how you can help. If you don't let your guide know your wants, desires, needs, or problems early on, they can't be expected to know them. If you're not enjoying your trip, tell your guide.

Guided Trips

Guided trips fall into two categories: wade and float. Wade trips add flexibility to your fishing day. Sometimes guides urge clients to split days between wading and floating. This is an effective strategy during the hot summer months, adding the flexibility in fishing the cooler hours of the morning or the late-evening hatches. This approach gives clients the opportunity to fish during the peak periods of the day. During a wade trip, the guide can give the client some very personalized instruction.

Float trips fall into two categories: belly boat and drift boat. Float trips are usually limited to two anglers per boat. Float fishing can be a memorable experience spending the day in a drift boat is a very rewarding experience because you access stretches of water that normally don't get fished. Float fishing requires accuracy. For the client, the trip can be a scenic and relaxing day, but not for the guide. It can be very frustrating for a guide, when clients miss golden opportunities due to poor casting technique. Casting from boats is an acquired skill with its own set of tricks. This type of fishing requires skilled anglers to cast at moving targets; its like wing shooting at pheasant or quail. Help yourself and your guide by practicing casting to targets before your trip. The better you can hit your target on the first cast, the more opportunities you will encounter in your fishing day.

During your float trip, the guide will put you in the best position to cast to a trout. You will only get one, maybe two, chances for casting at the trout. It is very aggressive fishing, with very few false casts. Concentrate on speed and accuracy.

Fishing with friends provides a lifetime of memories.

Chapter 36

The Hunt for Big Trout

Hunters have known for centuries how to pursue world-class trophies. But trout fishermen aren't used to thinking in those terms. Big-trout specialists are fishermen who choose their water and their season very carefully. They put in long days and nights on the water, in some of the worst conditions.

As a fly-fishing guide, I've seen why some anglers have better success with trophy trout than others. Fishermen that do their homework prior to the season, usually fair better throughout the year. To be successful at catching above-average trout, here are some secrets that can help you purse the trophy of a lifetime.

Read Water

It's important to learn to read water: lakes, rivers, and ponds. Trophy-size trout hold in different feeding lies than average-size trout. Learn to study the water you fish. When fishing large rivers, concentrate on edge cuts, seams, and obstructions. Most river fishermen understand that trout feed behind rocks or other visual obstructions, but also look for seams formed by current flows or obstructions in the water. If you fish lakes, study the rise of trout. Even in lakes or ponds there are obstructions under the water that hold large trout. Look for channels, steep drop-offs, shaded areas, stream inlets, and any other situation that produces food. If maps are available, study them. Trophy trout like places where there is cover, shade, and food.

Research

There are many resources available to trout fishermen. There are many seminars and clinics for fishing throughout the United States. Go to them and take notes. One of the best resources available is fishermen that fish the same water you do. Find out who catches a lot of big fish and set up a meeting with them. They may not tell you about their private fishing spots, but ask about different methods, techniques, or flies. Other sources include talking to specialty fly shops, ask for a fishing guide's name that you could contact for information. Fishing guides are on the water almost every day and have an updated account of what is hatching and where fish lie. There are also books and magazines that can keep you updated.

Fishing high mountain lakes can provide surprising results.

Equipment

Before you leave to go fishing, spend some time looking over your equipment. Check your line for breaks or cracks. Make sure you have extra leaders or tippets. Over the years I've always been amazed at how many fishermen purchase a trip and at the last minute can't find some of their equipment. Make a list of all the equipment you need to take on your trip, and check it off as you pack it. Spend time casting before you go fishing. The mistake that ruins a fishing trip is poor casting, whether it's on a boat or on the shore. It's frustrating when you see trout working and can't make the cast. The second mistake is making the line on the reel come off in knots or tangled.

Landing and Fighting

When you have a large trout on, keep your rod tip pointed towards the fish. Be patient and don't horse the fish. Remember, this is what you've been waiting for so enjoy the moment, don't rush it. Don't allow slack to build up on your line. The best way to avoid this is by fighting the fish from the reel. As soon as the fish has been hooked, try to get the line reeled up without giving slack in the line. This also allows you the opportunity to set the drag tighter. Stay out of the sight of the trout as it approaches the shore. Expect the trout to make several strong runs away from you. As the trout nears the shore, you have to make a decision on landing the fish, either land it with a net or beach the fish. Whichever method you choose, don't give the fish a lot of slack in the line. Once the fish is beached or netted, grasp the trout by the tail and support the abdomen. Be careful not to hurt the gills and try to keep the trout in the water. When catching large trout you'll want to check your leader for wind knots and make sure your hooks are sharp.

Trophy-Class Water

As a hunter, you'll want to do your research on trophy-size trout and where they live. If you want a big trout, you need to go to places that have quality trout. In most states there are pamphlets that you can attain from the division of wildlife pointing out gold-medal water. There are many private waters that might hold large trout. You may have to pay a fee, but most places are worth it.

If you have a chance to attend clinics or sports shows, go to the presentations put on by fishermen who hunt big trout. Study their techniques for searching for big trout.

Food Source

Be selective about which flies you use. Big trout have a passion for big flies. If you go to a tailwater river you might be able to catch a big trout on a small dry fly. Most of the time, the general rule is big flies, big trout. Again, you must do some research on the river or lake you are going to fish. It's not easy to catch trophy-size trout, do your homework before you go. The following is a list of questions you should ask:

Fishing trophy-class waters can produce trophy-class trout.

- What are the most common food sources in the water?
- Do I know what insect is available, and at what time of day?
- What fly selection should I have, what sizes and colors?
- What techniques should I know?
- At what level or depth do they find most of the bigger trout?

Study Fishermen

One important technique most anglers rarely use is watching successful anglers catch trout. There have been many times when I go to a new body of water that I will watch other anglers' techniques, approaches, and strategies as they continue to catch trout. I also talk to the angler. Most fishermen love to talk to you about their success. Most anglers love to tell about the trout they're catching and why they're doing so well. Several questions to ask these succesful fishermen are: What is their approach, casting technique, retrieve method, and selection of flies? What water depth are they fishing? What part of the stream or lake is more productive?

Quality versus Quantity

If you are going to pursue big trout, you will be challenged by many external and internal variables. Ask yourself, is it okay to have caught one big trout, instead of many nice-sized trout? Am I looking for quality or quantity? You usually don't get both.

Hunting big trout is a game of patience. You must be able to handle all types of uncontrollable situations. Be patient. Big trout are big for a reason, they're smart. It could take a lot of time before you catch your first big trout.

You must think differently about your fishing. An angler exposed only to average fishing conditions becomes only average in skills, their skills are only developed for easy-to-catch trout. We have trained ourselves in casting, line handling, fly selection, reading the water, spotting, stalking, everything is geared for small and easy-to-catch trout. You have to want to catch more and bigger trout, then you must develop the necessary skills to find and catch them. You must push yourself to research, react, reason, and reflect on each opportunity you've had.

Every trout you catch must be hunted and handled just like it were the biggest trout you've caught. Developing a competitive relationship with trout is the first step to breaking the mold. Start training yourself with the proper techniques early. It's tough to break an old habit. To be an effective hunter, learn the following about trout: where they live, how they live, what they eat, and how to read rise forms on the water (and pick between the little trout and big trout). Take notes, use a small pair of binoculars to locate trout, and think like a hunter.

Here are some guidelines (not in any particular order) to help the average angler become a better-than-average angler: sneak into casting range, check your leader for knots or nicks, make sure your hooks are sharp, analyze the currents, decide where to place the fly, plan the fight before you hook the trout, pull the line off the reel before casting, and keep the false casts to a minimum.

Handling large trout takes years of practice.

Even if you don't use all of the information in this section, the more you work on performing the right techniques, the better you will become. It's better to practice perfect technique a couple times a year, than practice poor technique many times a year. The quest for trophy trout is a big commitment. It takes research, reaction, reason, and reflection to gain the insights needed to develop the skills of trophy-trout fishing.

Systems

What is a system? All great fishermen have a system they use when fishing. Many great fishermen use a variety of combinations of lines and flies to achieve success. Some people call them the 'tricks of the trade', but actually fishermen design the system they use to catch more and bigger trout.

The system I use is a combination. The first rule is to change the depth of the water in which you work the fly. To do that, I change the amount of weight added to my leader. If I am still not getting deep enough, I will change fly lines to a faster sink-tip full-sinking line. As I work the fly at different depths, it allows me to find where the trout are holding. I have found that it's not the fly, but the depth at which you fish the fly, that triggers a bite. I've seen people constantly change flies during hatchless periods, when the trout have just changed the depth at which their feeding. In most situations only a handful of flies are really ever needed.

The second rule is, if you are at the correct depth, then change your retrieve. Slow down the technique you're using. If you are on a river, try a drag-free drift.

Taking care of a trophy trout should always be your number-one priority.

Chapter 37

Big-Fish Tactics

As you begin your quest for the trophy of a lifetime, there are many new tactics you will want to learn. Trout will teach you many new tricks, if you are observant. Spend time watching and studying big fish and you will increase your learning curve very quickly. Where to start has always been a mystery. I hope I have solved a few mysteries for you.

Trout You Can See

Which fly do I use? Which color? Which size? Where do I start? How do I begin? Here's how I approach fishing for big trout. I break it down into two categories: trout I can see and trout I can't see. When fishing a new body of water, I look for structure. Study maps of the river or lake. I bring the maps with me as I scout the water, looking for different structure.

Once you see a fish, catching that fish becomes a matter of tactics, presentations, and skills. Begin by attracting the fish. Which flies will attract the trout? Normally you try to match the hatch. You can also use an attractor pattern to trigger the trout: you must trigger the trout to bite. Use your best presentation. Finally, hook, and land the trout. The major challenge is to get the fly to the fish without scaring it off. Any trout that knows a predator is after it will not be caught on a fly. If you spook the trout, leave it alone. Don't cast again; let the trout sit for a couple of hours.

When you approach a trout you can see, watch the fish's gill and fins. How does the trout react to your presence, or to your cast? Study! Next notice the trout's mood changes. Be careful, almost sneaky. When you cast, one good cast is all it takes, be accurate.

Trout You Can't See

The most challenging skill is finding trout you can't see. The key is to define all of the available options of the trout; for example, look for structure, springs, channels, shelter, feeding lies, and holding lies. You need to search methodically using maps and visual signs to establish a trophy-trout patterns. Take notes. Use your maps, GPS, and note-taking skills to outsmart the trout.

When you begin fishing cover the area methodically. Be precise. Being able to use an efficient system to fish and to recognize structure will often determine your success. Your

odds of catching a trophy trout are determined by how well you have prepared.

Trouts' Diet

As trout grow, many reach a size where they begin eating other fish instead of insects as a primary food source. Trout grow up primarily as insect eaters. Most of the time, fly fishermen are taught to imitate a specific insect on which trout are feeding. Sometimes this works, but sometimes not. Another tactic is to appeal to the trout's natural selection process.

The natural selection process is when the predator eliminates food sources that are weak, struggling, or clearly vulnerable during a certain stage of their life cycle. How many completely white insects or forage fish do you see? Not many. Why? They get eaten. I usually start with white or off-white patterns to trigger a strike. Think outside the box.

Fade-Off Theory

Have you ever had a trophy trout fade off from your fly at the last moment?

I've seen big trout fade off many times I believe the reason is that the angler sees the trout and slows down their retrieve of the fly. Another common mistake is to continue the speed of the retrieve without ever changing it. Remember, trout of this size prefer forage fish not insects. Rather than dead-drifting a fly like an insect, it's better for your fly to react to the presence of a predator that's "hot on its tail." Here are some common rules to follow:

First, the larger the fly, the easier it is for the trout to determine whether it's a natural. Second, most flies specifically imitate a forage fish; you will be more successful if you concentrate on what the fly does, not how it looks. Third, rather than trying to imitate a natural food source, trigger the fish's natural selection instinct.

Above all, your observations and skills will determine your angling success. Being able to predict, with some degree of certainty, what triggers a fish to take a fly brings fulfillment and joy to our lives. Continually fishing new lakes, rivers, different species, and new tactics will greatly improve your skills.

Chapter 38

Defeating Giant Trout

How many times have you heard someone say, 'the big one got away?' Many people have a story just like that. If that were always true, why would we even bother to pursue trout?

It's a sick feeling when the big trout gets away. I remember hooking a big cutbow trout somewhere in the fifteen-pound class, the fight went on for over twenty minutes. The big trout made four long runs, stressing every part of my equipment. Then, for no reason, my line went limp and there was no fish. I wanted to sit down and cry. I checked the line, the tippet, the hook, and I could see no reason for that trout to have broken off. Why? The truth is I may never really know what happened that day. But I have learned techniques that minimize the percentage of trout breaking off.

Minimize Errors

Sometimes fish get off for no good reason, they just break off. But most of the time trout break off because of our errors. There are ways to minimize those errors. When a trout gets away, it's usually due to one of three reasons: the tippet, the knot, or the hook.

The tippet can be weakened by cuts, fray, old material, or being left on the line too long. Replace your tippet every few trout. If you hook and fight a large trout for several minutes, replace the tippet when you're done. You must become disciplined in changing your tippets frequently. If you practice this procedure, weak tippets will not be a problem when you're fighting a big trout. Using high-quality tippet material is the best way to avoid most tippet problems.

Minimizing your errors is key for catching monster trout.

The knot is critical between the tippet and the leader. Your knots must be perfect. This is one phase of the game where you have full control. Use knots that have a high knot-strength percentage. The time you spend learning the strongest knots is worth that trophy of a lifetime.

The hook is a key element in the fight. The hook can straighten out, get torn from the jaw, not set in a good place, or fall out. All of these problems can happen at one time or another. Most of the time trout break free because there is slack in the line and the hook falls out. Keeping your line slack-free is the key. You have to hustle when reeling the line onto the reel or strip the line while the trout is creating slack. Another reason you might lose a trout is because the hook comes out when the trout jumps. Study the chapter on landing and fighting trout.

Pressure to Win

What kind of pressure should you put on the trout? How hard should you pull on the line? The best answer to these questions is apply as much pressure as possible without breaking the tippet or knot. The truth is, most anglers don't know *how* to apply the proper amount of pressure or what *kind* of pressure to apply.

C-Stroke

There is one way to apply pressure to slow the trout down. I call it the C-stroke. The C-stroke fighting procedure was designed to quiet trout down after they make their big run. When you set the hook, a big trout panics and immediately takes off for deep water or shelter for protection. The purpose of C-stroking is to gain back line and put consistent pressure on the fish. It involves gaining line back with short

Using the C-stroke technique provides astounding results.

Getting a big trout to the net requires skill and technique.

quick pumps; you actually create a C with the rod. The rod tip should be about a foot from the water. As you reel the line, the tip goes toward the water. Reel the rod tip about six to eight inches to the water. Then lift the rod so the tip is about a foot from the water. The tip should never be up more than a fraction of a second. The thought is to pump, then crank, pump, then crank. Then reel again, repeating the process. It is taking little short strokes. The C-stroke is designed to take short strokes gaining line on a big trout. As you fight a trout with the C-Stroke the fish will actually calm down and become easier to land.

Many fishermen make the mistake of holding the rod tip too high while fighting a trophy trout. When your rod is straight in the air you apply the least amount of pressure on the fish. It will take longer for you to successfully net the trout. Pulling straight on the fish creates the most pressure, but it takes away the power of the rod to fight the fish. The best rod position lies between the two. It allows you to pressure the fish while still using the rod to slow down those sudden runs. It works if you practice.

My theory is you want to apply maximum pressure without hurting your tackle or the fish. The quicker you land a big fish, the better your chances of reducing post-release mortality. The sooner you land a fish the fewer things can go wrong. When you first hook a trout, the trout goes crazy running, jumping, and head shaking, or by just pulling. After this the trout will settle down and the fight will take place. After the trout makes its initial run, I start C-stroking the trout to submission. The reason for this is to force the fish to feel like it just sprinted a race and needs a break. Anaerobic muscle fatigue sets in with the trout. I believe if you never let the trout take a break, it means you can't rest either. You will be amazed at how quickly the trout can be landed. Most anglers don't understand the massive amount of pressure you can apply with tackle and the right fighting action. Most anglers just want to hold the rod tip straight up and lean back, bad habit.

You won't lose the fish of a lifetime if you remember the critical parts of fighting big trout. You'll sleep better if you land a big fish in a drag-screeching battle of emotion, instead of having to tell another story of how the big one got away.

Chapter 39

Fly-Fishing Tips

The following is a list of the twenty most important fly-fishing tips you should know. Review and understand the importance of each tip. As you get better in each of these areas, you will become a much better fly-fisherman.

1. You must have the stamina and perseverance to handle all types of weather conditions at different times of the day.
2. Food moves to trout in rivers. Trout move to food in lakes.
3. Fish by the four Rs: Research, Reason, React, and Reflect.
4. Understanding the aquatic insects, where you fish, and the depth at which they live, will greatly enhance your success.
5. Be ready and able to change tactics and techniques depending on the conditions.
6. Safety should be your top priority.
7. Develop perfect habits; treat every trout you catch as the trout of a lifetime.
8. Be able to cast your fly to different targets in different situations.
9. Look for good food-producing areas first.
10. Keep a fishing log. Past data is invaluable to future success.
11. Water temperature is the key to trout behavior.
12. Be able to recognize when to change fly patterns, lines, leaders, and presentations, which can change by the minute, hour, day, week or by the season.
13. Little trout may feed all day, but big trout don't. Trophy trout have certain feeding habits, learn them.
14. When you hook a trout, it's what you do that determines the outcome.
15. Wind knots weaken leaders. Don't take the chance, always re-tie.
16. Trout are usually visual feeders. Flies constructed of materials that breathe and move naturally will trigger a trout's feeding instincts.
17. Ninety percent of what trout eat lives under water.
18. Weather affects trout behavior. A change in weather will usually create a change under water.
19. The leader and tippet are usually the most over looked part of the tackle. Leaders can make the difference between success and failure.
20. It's not how far you strip the fly on the retrieve, but the speed of the fly that determines the success.

John Welfelt makes camp high in the Alaskan wilderness, where mistakes can be life threatening.

Chapter 40

Travel Tips

Fishing destinations are all different, each will present its own set of challenges. Because of all the different variables possible, it's important you research each destination. If you plan on flying make sure you check with the airlines for any travel restrictions. The following is a list of tips that has helped me continually as I prepare for each trip.

Use the Internet for research. You can find quite a bit of information about fly shops, water conditions, hatches, local hotels, guides, outfitters, restaurants, etc.

Contact fly shops in the area you will be visiting. This will help you cross reference the information you have from the Internet. If you are planning on using a guide or outfitter call them before you leave and get the latest scoop on the fishing. The earlier you book a trip, the better your chance of securing a top-rate guide before they are booked for the season.

Always plan for the worst possible conditions. I believe it's better to have too much gear than not enough. Always expect the worst weather. Many times, the week before you arrive the weather has been perfect, then when you arrive the weather is terrible, be prepared.

Ask about license or rod fees. Prepare to budget a certain amount of money towards these fees. Have extra money available for the unexpected license or rod fee. Many times I've gone places where the weather changed our plans on where we could fish.

Try to book your plane ticket as early as possible. Ask for an aisle seat (between rows 15 to 20), you will be able to get off earlier and there will be plenty of overhead storage. If you need more leg room, try to book an exit row seat. Go to the airport early; carry small-denomination bills for tips, snacks, and drinks. Purchase strong luggage tags. If your bags are lost, the luggage tags will help you with the identification of your bags.

Pack your luggage wisely. At the end of this chapter is a check list that I use on all my trips. The list has Consistently helped me to remember all essential items.

Be flexible. Not everything goes the way you planned. Always prepare for the worst. Control your emotions as situations arise.

Be realistic with your fishing trip. Besides catching fish, try to learn more about the water or area your're fishing. Take up photography, or keep an accurate journal. You can do everything right and never land a fish. Too many people go with high expectations and it ruins the trip.

Contact the shop, guide or outfitter before you leave. Ask about the right type of flies to bring and their color.

The color will be different on different rivers, lakes and at different times of the year. Ask about which type of fly line you should bring.

Purchase a strong, waterproof duffle bag. I also pack all my gear in large plastic bags. You can't have enough plastic bags along to store dirty clothes, trash or other items.

Before leaving on your trip check with your insurance company. Purchase travel insurance. Depending on your insurance company, the process can be very pain free. Many times I have relied on the insurance to cover the expense of rods, cameras and many other hard-to-replace items. Don't leave home without it.

Be smart about traveling through different airports and different towns. Don't show off your money. Leave expensive jewelry at home. Don't behave like a rude tourist. Be respectful of other people and their property. Avoid going with strangers that you have not checked out. Leave all your valuables in the hotel safe. Hide some money on you, just in case your room is robbed.

Travelling to far-away destinations requires careful planning and research.

Critical Items

- Itinerary
- Motel Reservations
- Rental Car Reservations
- Plane Tickets
- GPS
- Wallet
- Cash
- Credit Cards
- Travelers Checks
- Passport/Birth Certificate
- Proof of Insurance
- Licenses/Permits
- Cellular Phone/Charger
- Phone Numbers
- Copies of all paperwork
    (visa, passport, etc.)
- Maps/Directions
- Guidebooks
- Polarized Glasses
- Waterproof Bag

Clothing

- Fishing Shirts
- Travel Shirts
- Pants, long and short
- Belt
- Underwear
- Long Underwear
- Socks
- Swimsuit
- Towel
- Jacket
- Rain Gear
- Gloves
- Hats
- Shoes/Boots/Sandals
- Garbage bags

Toiletries

- Toothbrush
- Toothpaste
- Soap
- Shampoo
- Comb/Brush
- Deodorant
- Razor and Blades
- Shaving Cream
- Toilet Paper
- Medicine/Pills
- Fingernail Clippers
- Hand and Body Lotion

Fishing Gear

- Rods
- Reels
- Leatherman tool
- Journal
- Tackle
- Camera/Film/Batteries
- Waders
- Wading Boots
- Forceps
- Fishing Vest
- Flies
- Net
- Flashlight/Batteries

First Aid

- Bandages/Gauze
- Tweezers
- Antibacterial Lotion
- Pain-relief Medicine
- Anti-Itch Lotion
    (calamine, cortisone)
- Rolaids/Tums
- Cough Drops
- Throat Lozenges
- Carmex/Chapstix
- Dramamine/Bonine
- Neosporin
- Sunscreen

Other Items:_____

_____

_____

_____

_____

_____

_____

_____

_____

_____

_____

_____

_____

_____

_____

_____

_____

_____

_____

Chapter 41

Fly-fishing Journal

Why keep a fly-fishing journal? One of the most important aspects of fly-fishing is keeping a journal. If you take just a few moments at the end of your outing to record the information that is important to you, it can make a world of difference later on. Try to get into the habit of completing your journal as soon as you put your equipment away, while the experiences are still fresh in your mind.

A journal can help you remember information you would have forgotten over time. The journal can be used as a reference for information on productive times of the year, times of day, successful techniques and fly patterns, hatches, weather and water conditions, and much more. The journal can be a shortcut to possibly duplicating your success.

A journal should have many components, with several categories. The journal demonstrated in this manual is very comprehensive, you don't need to record all of the information, but it might help you remember certain information for future reference. This sample is very user friendly; it requires just checking off the appropriate information in different categories.

Keeping a journal provides data that can illustrate tendencies year after year.

Fly-Fishing Journal

Day_____Date_____Time_____

Specific Location_____

❏ River ❏ Stream ❏ Reservoir ❏ Lake ❏ Pond

Weather Conditions

Sky: ❏ Sunny ❏ Partly Cloudy ❏ Overcast
Moisture: ❏ Rain ❏ Thunder ❏ Sleet ❏ Snow
Wind: ❏ Light ❏ Moderate ❏ Gusts ❏ Strong
Wind Direction: ❏ North ❏ South ❏ East ❏ West

Temperature

Air Temp:_____Time:_____   ❏ a.m. ❏ p.m.
Water Temp:_____Time:_____   ❏ a.m. ❏ p.m.

Barometer

Reading: _____Time:_____   ❏ a.m. ❏ p.m.

Moon Cycle: ❏ New ❏ 1/2 ❏ Full ❏ 11/2

Solunar Time: ❏ Sun Rise ❏ Sun Set ❏ Moon Rise ❏ Moon Set ❏ Moon Up ❏ Moon Down

Water Conditions

Level: ❏ Low ❏ Medium ❏ High
Clarity: ❏ Dirty ❏ Cloudy ❏ Clear
Speed: ❏ Slow ❏ Medium ❏ Fast
Depth: ❏ 1-3 ft ❏ 3-5 ft ❏ 5-7 ft ❏ 7+ft

Location

River: Riffle_____Run_____Pool_____Tail____Other_____
Lake: Inlet_____Outlet_____Channels_____Shallows_____Weedbeds_____
Cliffs_____Drop-offs_____Other_____

Type of Rises

❏ Sip ❏ Head and Tail ❏ Splash ❏ Tailing ❏ Other_____

Fly Line:

Floating_____Clear_____Sink Tip_____Sinking_____Tippet Size_____Other____

Methods

❏ Sawyer ❏ Brooks ❏ Leisenring Lift ❏ Reach/Mend ❏ Greased Tippet
❏ Heave and Leave ❏ Strip/Tease ❏ Popping ❏ Hand Twist ❏ Other_____

Insect Activity

Collected Insects:_____Reference Numbers:_____
Hatch Type:_____Hatch Time:_____

Fishing Success

Species/#'s: ❏ Rainbow ❏ Brown ❏ Brook ❏ Cutthroat ❏ Other_____
Best Pattern: Name_____Size_____Color_____
Best Fish: Length_____Girth_____Weight_____Species_____
Time of catch:_____

What I have learned:

_____

_____

Notes:

Suggested Reading

Borger, Gary, *Presentation*. Tomorrow River Press. 1995.

Brooks, Charles E., *Nymph Fishing for Larger Trout*. Crown Publishers Inc. 1976.

Canty, Del, *Del Canty's Bellyboat Bible*. Matterhorn Printing and Design Co. 2000.

Cordes, Ron and Kaufmann, Randall, *Lake Fishing With A Fly*. Frank Amato Publications. 1984.

Eaton, Julie., *A Fly Rod and A Trout*. Scott Fly Rod Company. 1996.

Humphrey, Joe, *Joe Humphrey's Trout Tactics*. Stackpole Books. 1981.

Petralia, Joesph F., *Flyfishing*. Sierra Outdoor Products Co. 1994.

Perse, Richard M. II, *Pediatric First Aid for Child Care Professionals*. Heartsmart. 1994.

Rosenbauer, Tom, *Prospecting for Trout*. Dell Publishing. 1993.

Soucie, Gary, *Traveling With Fly Rod and Reel*. Henry Holt and Company. 1995.

Streitz, Ben, Bauer, Parker and Steruberg, Dick, *Trout*. Cowles Creative Publishing, Inc. 1988.

Talleur, Dick, *Fly Fishing For Trout*. Lyons and Burford Publishers. 1987.

Van Vliet, Jon, *Fly-Fishing Equipment and Skills*. Cy DeCosse Incorporated. 1996.

Van Vliet, Jon, Sternberg, Dick and Taieszen, David L., *Fly Fishing for Trout in Streams*. Cowles Magazine Company. 1996.

Whitlock's, Dave, *Guide to Aquatic Trout Foods*. Nick Lyons Books. 1982.